◊ *DIAMOND JUBILEE* ◊

Presented to

Mr D.A.V. Aldridge

by the Directors and Management
of Gleneagles Hotel
to commemorate the Hotel's
Diamond Jubilee in 1984

Gleneagles Hotel

GLENEAGLES HOTEL

DIAMOND JUBILEE
SOUVENIR BOOK
1924 · 1984

CONTENTS

A DREAM COMES TRUE 4
From one man's imagination, a new hotel concept is born

A COURSE FOR GOLFERS 18
The Gleneagles courses are meant to be enjoyed by all

INTO THE 21ST CENTURY 32
The hotel expands into a futuristic leisure resort

I REMEMBER GLENEAGLES HOTEL 42
Reminiscences of guests and staff

PUBLISHED FOR GLENEAGLES HOTELS PLC BY
Joint Marketing & Publishing Services Limited,
Newcombe House, Notting Hill Gate, London W11 3LQ
PUBLISHER
Philip Burley
TEXT BY
Jeremy Bruce-Watt
EDITOR
Milton Shapiro
PRODUCTION
Jeff Allen
PRINTED IN ENGLAND BY
Quadrant Print, London
BOUND BY
Green Street Bindery, Oxford
TYPESETTING
Century Old Style by Accent Graphics, London

ACKNOWLEDGEMENTS
Thanks are due to the following for help and advice received in the preparation of this book:
The management and staff of Gleneagles Hotel; the management of Gleneagles Hotels plc; Mr James Bannatyne, MBE, General Manager of the hotel from 1970 to April 1982. Mr Harry Jack, Edinburgh; Iain Crawford, Edinburgh; former guests and members of staff who have contributed, especially Miss Dorothy Crawford, who went to considerable trouble to record her reminiscences.

Further copies priced £9.50 may be obtained from the hotel.

End paper illustration of Gleneagles Hotel by Joseph Pike, circa 1925.

FOREWORD

"Today the very name Gleneagles conjures up pictures of all that is best in Scotland.

It is therefore my pleasure to write a foreword to this special book commemorating the Diamond Jubilee of one of Scotland's great institutions, Gleneagles Hotel.

It is the only 5 star hotel in Scotland and is recognised worldwide as one of the most important assets of the flourishing Scottish tourist industry.

Here is a unique asset: Gleneagles. Nestling in Perthshire in some of Scotland's most beautiful countryside, it is a byword everywhere for high cuisine and recreation in elegant surroundings. It is a reputation which has gone around the world.

Gleneagles has succeeded and will continue to succeed because of its traditions in excellence. Second best is not good enough.

Over the years world leaders, world class golfers and household names like Bing Crosby and Bob Hope have savoured the delights of this hotel. Indeed I am surprised they never made a film "The Road to Gleneagles".

Despite its years Gleneagles continues to grow and set even higher standards which few can match. The dynamic young team which leads this establishment are a shining example to many other industries – they make use of all things modern: technology expertise and methods – along with the best trained people. With that recipe they can keep ahead of any competition anywhere.

Safe in the hands of a sound Scottish company I am confident that all concerned with Gleneagles Hotels plc may just find that life begins at 60."

George Younger.

Rt. Hon. George Younger MP,
Secretary of State for Scotland

"THE EVER-CHANGING VISTAS OF HILL AND GLEN AND SHINING RIVER MADE A DEEP IMPRESSION ON MATHESON, AND WHEN HIS HOLIDAY CAME TO AN END HE WENT HOME WITH AN INSPIRATION."

GLENEAGLES HOTEL in Perthshire, on the southern edge of the Scottish Highlands, was created sixty years ago out of one man's dream. It is now an incomparable reality for countless thousands who have journeyed to it from all over the world.

The very name Gleneagles has a majestic and romantic ring. It speaks of a proud people and the grandeur of a rugged and historic countryside and, in the context of the modern luxury hotel, of a renowned hospitality, good fellowship amongst its guests and unrivalled facilities for sportsmen.

From the moment it opened its doors for the first time on Saturday, 7th June, 1924, Gleneagles Hotel took its place amongst the truly great leisure palaces of Europe and the world.

The Gleneagles Hotel story actually begins in the year 1910, when a senior Scottish railway executive named Donald A. Matheson spent a memorable holiday in the tree-studded river valley known as Strathearn.

Matheson was a small man of charming personality and imaginative ideas. He had had a long career in railways, spanning the time of the fierce competition and rapid expansion of the late nineteenth century. After service with the London and North Western Railway and the Lancashire and Yorkshire Railway he joined the Caledonian Railway Company—a prosperous and enterprising Scottish group which promoted the largest of all the nineteenth century railway operations in Scotland. At first he was resident engineer, then engineer-in-chief. In 1910, the year of his highly significant holiday, he had just been made general manager of his company, thus assuming the considerable influence and initiative of the position.

The Caledonian railway track already ran through Strathearn on its way from Edinburgh and Stirling to Perth, the county town. The ever-changing vistas of hill and glen and shining river made a deep impression on Matheson, and when his holiday came to an end he went home with an inspiration. This was the creation of "a Georgian Hotel or country house, built in the style of a palace, to attract and cater for the British travelling class"—placed in the seclusion of the Strathearn pinewoods, surrounded by the flowering wilderness of heather and gorse that is a typical Scottish moor.

Donald Matheson set to work to convert and convince his fellow directors. It seems that they quickly accepted his vision with an enthusiasm matching his own.

THE POST, SATURDAY, JUNE 7, 1924.

OPENING OF MAGNIFICENT HOTEL AT GLENEAGLES.

OUTDOOR SPORT AND INDOOR ENTERTAINMENTS.

New Gleneagles a Luxurious Hotel

Establishment in Scottish Highlands Opened Early in June in Many Ways Similar to Westchester Biltmore—Foundation Laid in 1914

THE BULLETIN

GOLF DE LUXE

Opening of Magnificent Hotel at Gleneagles

OPULENCE AND ELEGANCE

SPECIAL TO "THE BULLETIN"

THE DUNDEE ADVERTISER

BROADCAST FROM GLENEAGLES

Novel Opening of New Hotel

COUNTRY CLUB FOR SCOTLAND

Fresh Trout on the Premises

THE SCOTSMAN, SATU

NEW SCOTTISH RESORT.

GLENEAGLES SCHEME COMPLETED.

RAILWAY COMPANY'S ENTERPRISE.

GLENEAGLES golf course has attained unto world fame suddenly. It did not become great. It did not acquire a reputation gradually. Rather it was born great. Some imaginative mind discovered that Nature in one of her most pleasant and accommodating moods had fashioned those heather-clad hills and moors in a way which yielded easily to the treatment of the golf course architect. The result is two courses which are acclaimed among the best in Britain. In like manner there was conceived the idea of making Gleneagles a place to stay as well as a place to play. That aspiration has now been realised, and Gleneagles Hotel this week accommodates its first visitors.

The opulence, elegance and grand style of the new Gleneagles Hotel brought Fleet Street out in superlatives. Above left, one of the hotel's first postcards. Left: artist's sketches made for the 1924 opening evoke nostalgic memories of the Twenties.

The entire scheme of colour, lighting effects, and furnishing of the Gleneagles Hotel and the supervision of the work in progress was entrusted to

Muggeridge

Consultant for Furnishing and Decoration
42, Berners Street
LONDON, W.1
Telephone Museum 2436

who specializes in creating new ideas in furnishing, decoration, lighting, and colour, and in purchasing the necessary furniture and fabrics from the most advantageous British and Continental sources

Commissions recently executed or in progress for the following

Gleneagles Hotel :: Perthshire
Hotel Bristol :: Beaulieu
Hotel Metropole, Monte Carlo
Hotel Metropole :: Cannes
Commercial Bank of London
Midnight Follies, Hotel Metropole, London:
Restaurant, Hotel Victoria, London:
London Midland & Scottish Railway Co
AND THE
Garden Club, Grill Room and Grand Restaurant, at the British Empire Exhibition, Wembley, 1925

Interviews by appointment only

The site chosen was a gentle slope on a part of what was known locally as The White Muir of Auchterarder, two miles west of the village of the same name. The outlook was magnificent. To the south the eye travelled the 25-mile-long range of the Ochil Hills. The foothills of the great Grampian Mountain chain formed a barrier to the north. On a clear day the distinctive outline of Ben Lomond rose to the west. Eastwards the view extended 40 miles down the Strath towards the sea.

In 1913 a company known as Gleneagles Ltd. was formed for the purpose of constructing and operating the proposed hotel and golf course, with the Caledonian Railway Company agreeing to subscribe up to £25,000 to help it on its way. Building began at once, using large quantities of stone taken from a disused railway viaduct. A service railway was built from the nearby station to the site for the transport of materials. (In later years this was used to convey guests in passenger coaches literally to the hotel's back door).

In the autumn of 1914, after the outbreak of the First World War, the whole project was halted—and for the next nine years the embryo hotel, already a landmark visible for miles, stood as a forlorn and roofless shell. Doubts must have arisen as to whether it would ever be finished, but work resumed in 1922 and was completed in record time. It included the bringing of an electricity supply sixteen miles from Bridge of Allan, and water two miles from a reservoir.

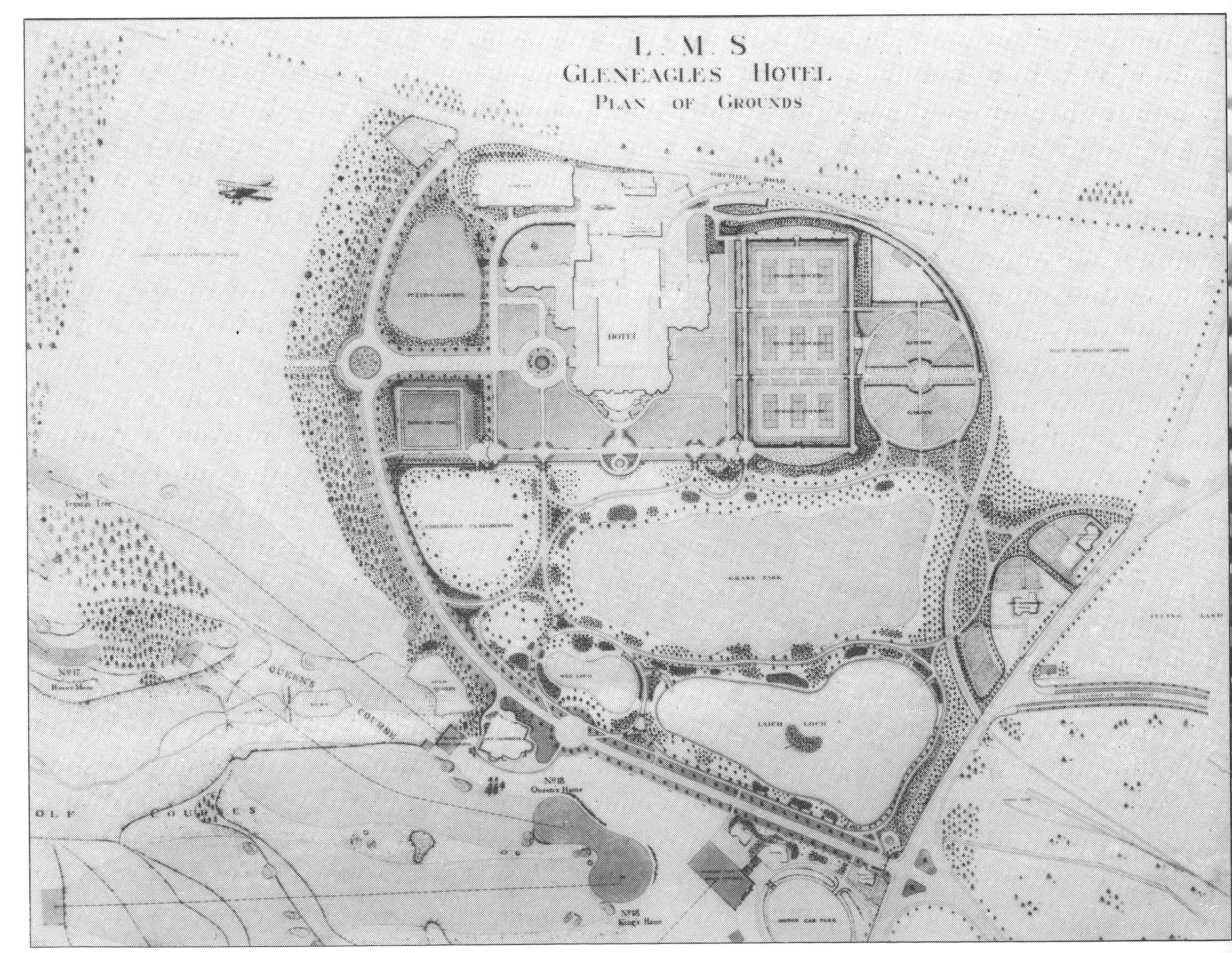

From the first, Gleneagles Hotel did everything in style, from its hotel bus, to bringing in the first grouse by motorcycle, to its Grand Design (page left). At top, Donald A. Matheson (at left) looks at one of the earliest awards of the Silver Tassie.

On 1st July, 1923, The Caledonian Railway Company became part of The London, Midland and Scottish Railway. Donald Matheson, whose star was still in the ascendant, was appointed deputy general manager of the Scottish section.

With the hotel almost ready to open, there occurred an administrative hitch. Gleneagles Ltd. found themselves unable "for financial and other reasons" to complete the erection of the hotel and the laying out of the allied golf courses. An Act had to be passed through Parliament enabling the railway company to take over the land and maintain the fairways themselves.

A year later, on Saturday, 7th June, 1924, Donald Matheson saw his dream come true.

In passing, the story of how both railway station and hotel came to acquire their name makes interesting reading.

At the time when the first plans were being drawn up the station nearest to the chosen site bore the unromantic name of Crieff Junction—being the point at which the track formerly owned by a small local company met that of the Scottish Central Railway. (Both were later absorbed by the Caledonian Railway Company).

As this name was quite unsuited to the disembarkation point for a major luxury hotel, the directors searched the local map for an alternative—and came upon the obvious choice. There was, however, an immediate difficulty. Gleneagles, although only two miles away, was a territory quite separate from the rolling open country of Strathearn. It was and is a wild and precipitous place with a long history. The house of Gleneagles, the

Guests at Gleneagles Hotel helped fill the pages of the society columns. Top left: Arthur Towle, who hired Henry Hall to play for the hotel's opening, with novelist Margery Lawrence, announcing their wedding plans. That's Margery frolicking in the snow at the hotel. Above: Lloyd George delivers a stroke on the course. Below, from left: The Hon. Charles Baillie Hamilton (Secretary to Stanley Baldwin) Lady Dorothy MacMillan, Mr Robert Boothby, M.P. (Secretary to Winston Churchill) and the then Capt. Harold MacMillan, M.P. Photo taken at Gleneagles Hotel in 1926.

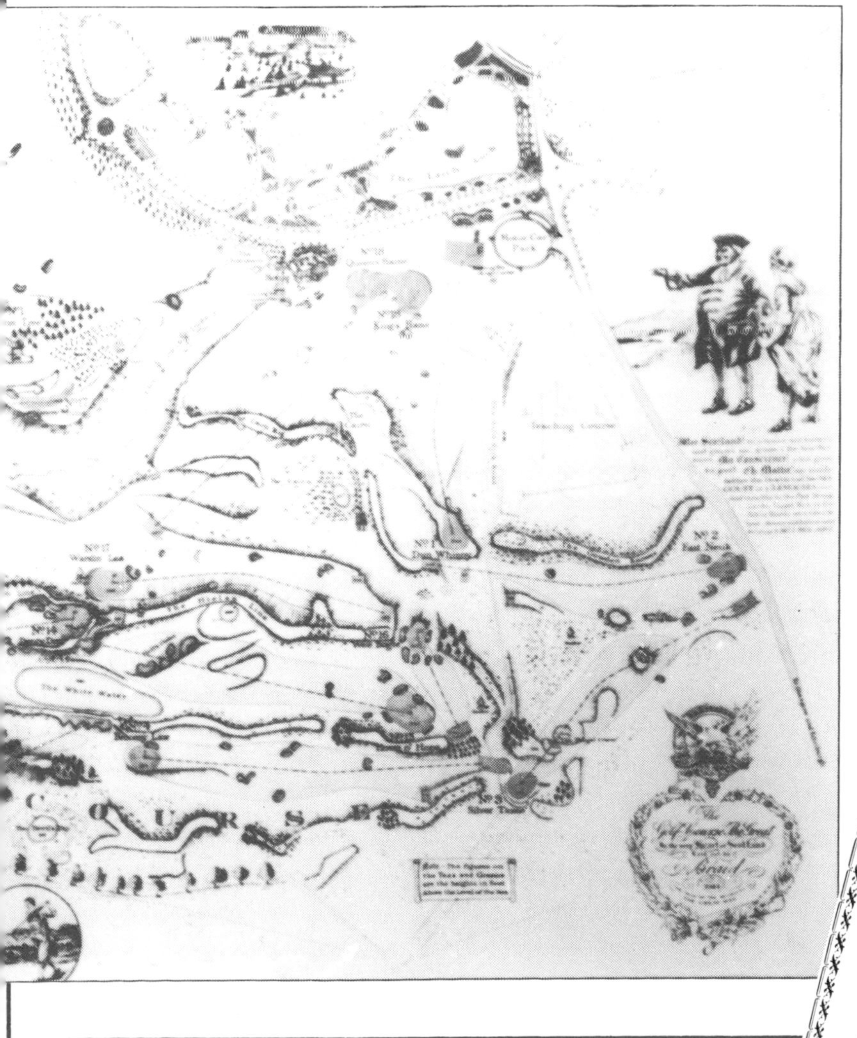

family seat of the Haldanes of Gleneagles, was built in or before 1624 from the stones of an even earlier castle. (A famous Scots poem tells of revels at Gleneagles Castle in the boyhood of King James V in the early 1500s).

Any new use of the name by modern commercial outsiders was obviously a matter for consultation with the family, which had owned the estate for over seven hundred years.

The company proceeded optimistically. The Board and Committee minutes record a meeting of the Traffic Committee in Glasgow on 5th September, 1911. Under the heading "Crieff Junction" it is noted: "Read letter from Mr. Pettigrew suggesting that the name of Crieff Junction Station be changed to Gleneagles. It is recommended that the suggestion be given effect to." Then is added the ominous word: "Postponed."

It seems that after diplomatic overtures to Lord Camperdown, then proprietor and custodian of the family lands and title, with assurances as to the prestigious nature of the company's project, he gave his consent to a change in the name of the station. Permission to apply the name Gleneagles to the hotel, however, was never either sought or granted.

Four years later, in the midst of all the euphoria, the topic was raised again in no uncertain manner. In September, 1928, Mr Brodrick Chinnery-Haldane of Gleneagles wrote to the *Daily Record* in Glasgow:-

"I am well aware that, owing to the outrageous and uncalled-for attempt made by the officials of the late Caledonian Railway Company and by what the L.M.S. have thereby succeeded to, the public have been led to think that the L.M.S. company *own* Gleneagles.

"...Our family has owned Gleneagles since the 12th century, and you will appreciate that we very much resent being mixed up with a modern railway hotel.

"...You lately published pictures in connection with the burial of Lord Haldane at my private chapel here, and certainly this was correctly described as at Gleneagles, but from your description of the opening of the new golf course, people might think that he was buried on the golf course, so you will see the absurdity of calling the golf course Gleneagles."

GLENEAGLES HOTEL.

LAIRD AND MISUSE OF NAME.

FAMILY RIGHT.

With reference to the opening of a new golf course at Gleneagles Hotel on Monday last, the Editor of the "Daily Record" has received the following letter from Mr. Brodrick Chinnery-Haldane of Gleneagles :—

The golf course which was opened was not at Gleneagles, but at the L.M.S. Hotel connected with the misnamed station of Gleneagles. Neither station hotel, nor either golf course i[...] point on Gleneagles[...] of the estate[...]

The fame of the new 'dream' hotel spread far and wide via publicity, word-of-mouth and advertising. Below left is an advertisement that appeared in Town & Country in New York in 1928. Meantime controversy over the Gleneagles name continued via Mr Chinnery Haldane (upper left). See text.

Donald Matheson himself attracted a share of the family displeasure.

"Mr Matheson, who more than anyone else was responsible for the misuse of my name, wrote more than once to assure me that 'nothing was further from the minds of the company than to attempt to take the honoured name of Gleneagles', yet he actually had the audacity to mark the forks and spoons made for the railway hotel with the plain word 'Gleneagles'—not 'Hotel'."

In the circumstances, considerable sympathy rests with the Haldane family, but although a change of name was seriously considered by the L.M.S., it was by now too firmly rooted as a consequence of "force majeure."

Following the opening gala on that summer Saturday in 1924, the national Press greeted the new resort with extraordinary enthusiasm, hailing it as "The Playground of the Gods, The Switzerland of Scotland, and The Scottish Palace in the Middle of a Moor."

Correspondents marvelled at the details of the Gleneagles scene. The hotel had its own cold storage plant and bakery, with all baking and cooking done by electricity. There was equipment for washing four thousand dishes an hour. Particular interest was shown in the automatic potato peeler and egg boiler. A huge tank contained a supply of fresh trout.

Most of the furniture was British, if not Scottish, but other items had been gathered in from Italy, Belgium, France, Madeira and Canada. "If the hotel's carpets were to be taken out and laid end to end they would stretch almost from Dundee to Forfar—twelve miles of varying hues!"

In the dining room 300 guests sat at small tables. Two hundred couples filled the ballroom. On the upper floors 216 bedrooms offered accommodation for 350 visitors. The garage had space for 80 cars. In the American bar, cocktails poured from taps. Distinguished guests were assured by the management of protection from the Press.

Newspaper reports apart, the new Gleneagles Hotel was guaranteed national attention by the fact that the music at the opening ball was broadcast all over Britain by the BBC. This was regarded as a technical miracle and caused great excitement. The sound was amplified and put over a land line to Glasgow and transmitted from there. Hotel guests possessing wirelesses listened with astonishment to the dance music being played elsewhere within the same building.

"Mr Matheson was justly proud of the claim for Gleneagles that it was the first place in the Highlands to broadcast," said one reporter, although in fact the credit was due to someone else soon to become a household name in his own right.

Some months before, the Controller of LMS Hotel Services, Arthur Towle, had visited the Midland Hotel in Manchester and chanced to hear a remarkable performance by a young deputy pianist, improvising until the band was ready. Towle was so impressed that he asked him if he would like to conduct the orchestra at a new hotel he was opening soon in Scotland.

The name of the young man was Henry R. Hall. He was then twenty-six and accepted with alacrity. On arrival in Scotland it was he who contacted the BBC and suggested the broadcast, and so it came about that his Gleneagles Hotel Band, playing their signature tune "Come ye back to bonnie Scotland" was heard nationwide. (Programmes from Gleneagles Hotel thereafter became a twice-weekly event).

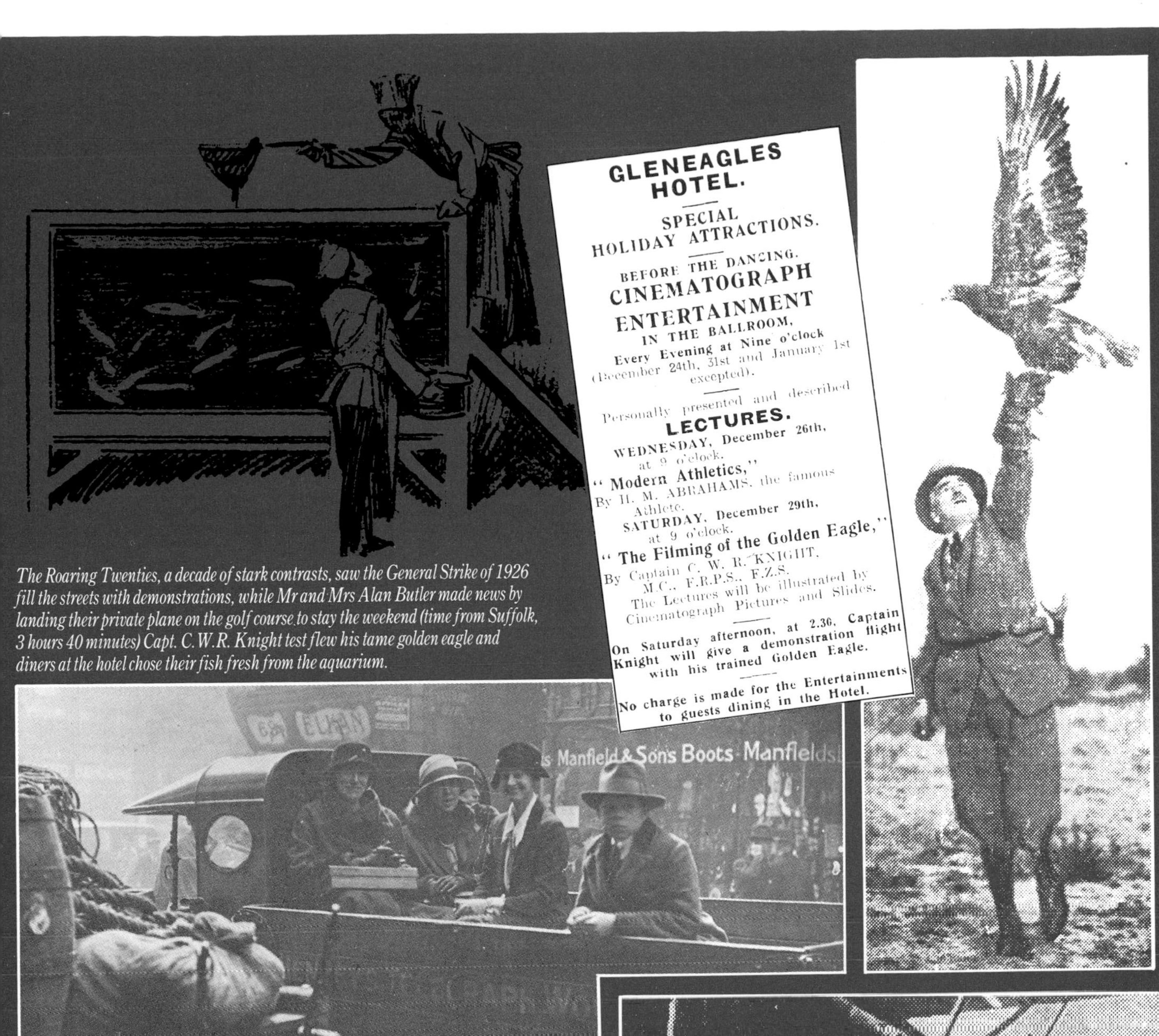

GLENEAGLES HOTEL.

SPECIAL HOLIDAY ATTRACTIONS.

BEFORE THE DANCING.

CINEMATOGRAPH ENTERTAINMENT

IN THE BALLROOM,

Every Evening at Nine o'clock
(December 24th, 31st and January 1st excepted).

Personally presented and described

LECTURES.

WEDNESDAY, December 26th,
at 9 o'clock.

" Modern Athletics,"
By H. M. ABRAHAMS, the famous Athlete.

SATURDAY, December 29th,
at 9 o'clock.

" The Filming of the Golden Eagle,"
By Captain C. W. R. KNIGHT, M.C., F.R.P.S., F.Z.S.

The Lectures will be illustrated by Cinematograph Pictures and Slides.

On Saturday afternoon, at 2.30, Captain Knight will give a demonstration flight with his trained Golden Eagle.

No charge is made for the Entertainments to guests dining in the Hotel.

The Roaring Twenties, a decade of stark contrasts, saw the General Strike of 1926 fill the streets with demonstrations, while Mr and Mrs Alan Butler made news by landing their private plane on the golf course to stay the weekend (time from Suffolk, 3 hours 40 minutes) Capt. C.W.R. Knight test flew his tame golden eagle and diners at the hotel chose their fish fresh from the aquarium.

Henry even wrote a piece of music for the occasion, entitled "Glen of Eagles," This was a medley of four tunes dedicated to James Braid, the renowned golfer who designed the first Gleneagles courses; Gordon Lockhart, the first Gleneagles golf professional; Arthur Towle; and the nearby village of Auchterarder.

Later, a book of sheet music was published under the title "Old Scottish Dance Tunes." These were strathspeys, reels and country dances arranged for the piano by J. Meredith-Kay, price 2s 6d. It showed the Gleneagles Hotel crest in the form of a clan badge complete with eagle, sprig of heather and motto: "Heich abune the Heich" (High above the High). The first strathspey was the tune entitled "Miss Haldane of Gleneagles."

Meanwhile, thousands of words were being written about Gleneagles every week—not only on the hotel but of the range of outdoor activities that formed part of its country house-party way of life, golf, tennis, shooting, fishing, even skating and tobogganing. Events which would have been unremarkable anywhere else made news because of where they were taking place.

One nameless celebrity was given headlines when he raced his Rolls-Royce against the L.M.S. train from London, stopped to eat three times on the way and managed to arrive at the hotel within ten minutes of the express.

Others made aviation history. In 1926 a Mr and Mrs Alan Butler flew their own aeroplane up from Suffolk and landed on the golf course to stay the week-end. "The journey took only three hours and forty minutes."

In 1928, a Mr J.G. Cramond piloted his own bi-plane from Croydon and nonchalantly joined his parents for lunch. Thereafter, "flying to the

The legendary Henry Hall and some of the original sheet music written for the hotel

Whilst winter sports were all the rage for social occasions, flying was becoming very much the thing at Gleneagles. Above, Mr. J.G. Cramond flew up from Croydon to join his parents at Gleneagles (September 1928) and at right, Capt. W.R. Bailey and Mrs. Muntz, described in The Daily Express of 1929 as "two keen fliers" arrived at the hotel for the Gleneagles Air Rally, equipped with golf clubs and tennis racquets.

Scottish Highlands," a hitherto unheard-of adventure, became commonplace. For the big Gleneagles Air Rally of 1929 pilots arrived with golf bags strapped to their planes.

By now the hotel complement of guests had become known as "The Gleneagles Three Hundred"—although at peak periods there were 380, looked after by 430 staff including 60 waiters and 75 in the kitchens.

Society pages seemed incomplete without glimpses of the plus-fours, the tennis whites, the furs and evening clothes of Gleneagles Hotel. "Seen at Gleneagles this week-end were..." Flocks of Americans arrived by sea in Glasgow. Their luggage included their cars.

"I cannot tell you half the ritualistic things people do here," enthused a writer in *The Westminster Gazette.* "They tea-dance in the gayest of sun lounges with windows opening to the Ochils and the glen. They mix-bathe in the swimming pool in costumes of a Deauville splendour. They play billiards and bridge and dance again in the ballroom of mirrors and gilt chairs and stage decorated with Japanese trellis.

"Then, exultant from the dance, they midnight bathe in the pool again under lamps that give a light white as sunlight. At the windows they smoke a pyjama cigarette, with the wine-like air from the Perthshire hills and the night and the stars playing about them."

For those who did not engage in sport there were the attractions of the surrounding countryside, which offers at close range some of the finest scenery in Scotland.

Not far to the west is the spectacular corner of the Highlands known as the Trossachs, a place of forests and lochs and wild, dramatic-looking hills—the setting for Sir Walter Scott's novels "Rob Roy" and "The Lady of the Lake." It also features in Robert Louis Stevenson's "Kidnapped." (David Balfour's epic flight through the turbulent eighteenth-century Highlands passed southwards to the Allan Water, a few miles west of the Gleneagles Hotel).

Of such, then, was the nature of the twenties and thirties at Gleneagles Hotel: golden times for golden people, a mecca for high society, a temple of the game of golf. Its brilliant social life continued unabated until in 1939 the war clouds gathered and the storm finally burst over Europe and the world.

For the grandest of British country hotels this meant closure, requisition by the Government and conversion into a convalescent hospital for the troops. An era had come to an end and Gleneagles was never to be quite the same again.

"Afore ye go"
BELL'S
SCOTLAND'S
NUMBER ONE
QUALITY
SCOTCH WHISKY
BELL'S
Old Scotch Whisky
EXTRA SPECIAL
RTHUR BELL & SONS plc., ESTABLISHED 1825 AND STILL AN INDEPENDENT COMPANY

"AS HE WAS IN THE HABIT OF PUTTING HIS OWN NAME TO THE HOLE HE CONSIDERED TO BE THE FINEST, THE THIRTEENTH ON KING'S IS CALLED BRAID'S BRAWEST,"

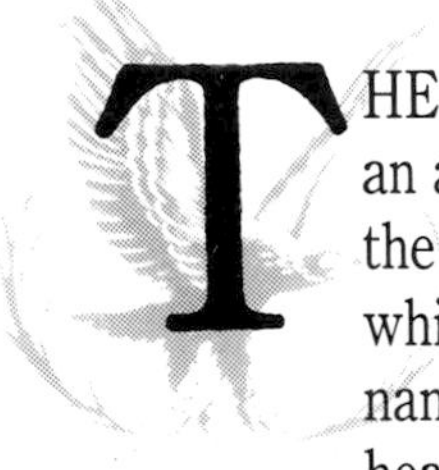

THE GREENS AT GLENEAGLES ARE PERFECT NOW. So proclaimed an advertisement in the *Golf Illustrated* of 1929. It was an exhortation by the White Star Line to Americans to cross the Atlantic and play on courses which, still in the early years of their existence, had become household names in the world of golf. GOLF AT GLENEAGLES was a regular headline and photographs showing players among heather-covered ridges topped with pine trees and backed by dramatic hills, proclaimed the Gleneagles Hotel courses without the necessity for a caption.

It was just before the First World War, while work was beginning on the construction of the hotel, that Donald Matheson looked around for a designer for two golf courses to be laid out in the hotel grounds. Appropriately, he approached one of the giants of the golfing world, James Braid.

Braid was then the highly respected professional at Walton Heath in London, but apart from that he was a member of the famous golfing "triumvirate" of Vardon, Braid and Taylor, and had been winner of the Open Championship five times between 1901 and 1910. He was a personality of great charm, physically very tall and heavily built—which made him a powerful adversary on the course—and he accepted Matheson's commission (in association with Major C.K. Hutchison) with enthusiasm.

King's and Queen's were thus created together out of a virgin wilderness of whins and heather, using horses, carts, picks and shovels. James Braid designed a large number of courses towards the end of his career (possibly the first professional to do so) but those at Gleneagles Hotel are surely his most celebrated, and he himself thought them his best work. As he was in the habit of putting his own name to the hole he considered to be the finest, the thirteenth on King's is called "Braid's Brawest."

King's and Queen's were open and played on sporadically during the war, but between 1918 and the opening of the hotel in 1924 their fame had begun to spread, making Gleneagles Hotel a place of golfing pilgrimage. "As many as fourteen men have been seen working at the same time on one green!" reported an awestruck visitor.

Gordon Lockhart was the first professional. He was a tall, handsome man, and well liked. He had several assistants: William Walker, Willie Callum and one very able lady, Bessie Young.

THE GREENS AT GLENEAGLES ARE PERFECT NOW

PLAY THE HISTORIC SCOTCH COURSES THIS SUMMER

The 17th Green at Gleneagles

Plan now to enjoy THE vacation you have been promising yourself since you first succumbed to the lure of the Ancient and Honorable. Think of teeing off in the land where bairns cut their teeth on niblicks and brassies, and the nineteenth hole still thrives — bonny Scotland, the gowfer's paradise!

Only that vast water hazard, the Atlantic, stretches between you and the land of your dreams—and that's easily played if you cross on a White Star, Red Star or Atlantic Transport liner. Great numbers of golf enthusiasts travel to Europe every summer on these luxurious ships. You will meet them on *yours* going over. They take the same pride in a superbly-appointed vessel that they do in a well-planned golf course. Instinctively they select the best among both.

In our fleets you have a choice of such famous liners as the ***Majestic*** (world's largest ship), ***Olympic, Homeric, Belgenland, Lapland, Pennland, Arabic, Adriatic, Baltic, Cedric, Minnewaska, Minnetonka,*** etc. —and two remarkable ships, the ***Minnekahda*** and ***Minnesota,*** that carry TOURIST Third Cabin passengers exclusively.

FREQUENT SAILINGS

WHITE STAR LINE

RED STAR LINE · ATLANTIC TRANSPORT LINE

INTERNATIONAL MERCANTILE MARINE COMPANY

For full information address No. 1 Broadway, New York, our offices elsewhere or authorized steamship agents.

View from the Gleneagles Hotel

Robinson

Below, left, Joe Kirkwood on the King's 18th during a 1925 tournament. Above: the legendary James Braid. Below, right teeing off at the 18th on the Queen's Course.

Among early players who came to take part in exhibition matches was Joe Kirkwood—a great favourite—who demonstrated trick shots, driving off from a watch instead of the sand tees then in use. On occasion he would even do the same from the faces of volunteers lying on the ground.

One whole group of golfers, intent on an idyllic week-end, came by special train from Euston, which also contained a piano, pianist, and all the ingredients of a hectic party.

The jewel in the Gleneagles golfing crown is still the King's Course—a majestic, airy arena hemmed by distant hills. From the time James Braid designed it this course has always offered a long, exhilarating and exacting game—and today this description is the more apt following judicious and imaginative alterations by Gleneagles Hotels p l c, who acquired the entire property in 1981.

Braid laid out King's at about 6,500 yards. Three years ago it was extended to almost 7,000 yards, with tees being moved, enlarged or added to. The thinking behind this operation was to contrive to maintain the characteristic difficulty that Braid had intended—bearing in mind that the hickory shafts and balls of gutta-percha have been superseded by today's steel shafts and high-powered golf balls.

As a result, King's remains a tough course in modern terms. It is also higher and more exposed than the others—the highest point on the twelfth green is just over 600 feet above sea level—and is more affected by strong winds. Fairways are generous but not over wide, and a player who misses is in dire trouble—probably into head high bushes and heather.

GLENEAGLES

Golf isn't golf unless the course is good. Whether you are a first-class player or merely moderate, a good course makes a good game. At Gleneagles the greens, fairway, rough and bunkers are so good that professional golfers describe Gleneagles golf as the finest in the world. The glory of Gleneagles golf is due to three things. The view—sixty miles of highland grandeur round you; mountains, heather, moorland, as far as you can see. The peacefulness—at no time are you harried by players on adjacent holes, because each hole seems to lie by itself, hidden away. And the variety—not one of the holes on the three separate courses faintly resembles another. Each offers new problems to unravel, new obstacles to surmount, and new testimony to your skill.

And the hotel at Gleneagles—as the rendezvous of smart folk from both sides of the Atlantic, Gleneagles hotel holds a hearty welcome for the Overseas Visitor. Gleneagles offers every comfort and every elegance of the big cities, among the lochs and glens and the heather—the luxury of London in the midst of the moorland.

Queen's — shorter, less taxing, eminently picturesque, giving the impression of privacy and seclusion.

Glendevon — making its own subtle demands on a player's skill. It opens and closes dramatically across the water.

The King's Course, jewel in the Gleneagles crown. A tough course, as Braid intended it to be.

King's is well bunkered. Its combined attributes make for a very tough but utterly memorable day.

If the King's course is grandly panoramic, the Queen's is outstandingly picturesque, shorter, less taxing. It incorporates a rush-filled lochan and a rustic bridge. Many of the holes are flanked by bushes and dark fir trees, so that the impression of privacy and seclusion is particularly powerful.

The summer of 1928 saw the opening of a third course of nine holes. This was known as "The Wee Course", stretched to 2,650 yards, and was designed by the head greenkeeper, George Alexander. His son and other members of the staff carried out most of the work themselves, using turf produced by the Gleneagles Hotel nursery. The Wee Course was lengthened to the full eighteen holes in 1974 and renamed Prince's. With appealing characteristics of its own — one of them being that the ball has to be hit *very* straight but never very far — this course has become particularly popular with families.

The newest course, Glendevon, was opened in 1980. Built on farmland, it is less hilly than the others — thus suiting those players who prefer an easier walk. Glendevon is quite different in character from the other three, and makes its own subtle demands on skill and sense of judgement — it opens and closes with two dramatic holes across water.

It goes without saying perhaps that all the courses, thanks to the dedicated attention of James Kidd, the estates manager, and Scott Walker, the head greenkeeper, and staff, are maintained in superb condition all the year round.

Even the damage caused by the harsh winter of 1978, when the courses were badly scarred by the ravages of frost and severe cold, has left no mark today.

No one is better qualified to reflect on the qualities of Gleneagles Hotel golf than the present professional, Ian Marchbank. Coming to Strathearn from Alan Glen's School and the R.A.F., he confesses to thirty years close acquaintance with the Gleneagles courses, interrupted only by four years on the almost equally renowned territory of Turnberry in Ayrshire.

It was a young Ian Marchbank (centre) who came to Gleneagles as pro in the 1960's. Bill Paterson (left) and Hugh McCorquodale were his assistants.

Ian Marchbank today, still very much the Gleneagles professional

Golfing fashion was a wee bit different back in 1928 when the Wee Course opened at Gleneagles (above) with an exhibition match between Gordon Lockhart of Gleneagles and James McDowell of Turnberry. At lower right there's James Braid himself, the man who designed the first Gleneagles courses. Photos right and lower left were contributed by Joseph Scherer (holding wood, below) a regular at Gleneagles in the late 20's.

"The Gleneagles courses are my favourites, of course. They're very unusual and very much loved. Every golf course has an atmosphere and an image and a character no less than the people who play on it, and it's said of these that if you're out on them on a fine day the world's worries simply disappear.

"The sense of seclusion here is complete. The only other human beings you see are those behind you if you turn round, or, if you look up, the players ahead of you. To the side there are only trees, bushes, heather, and a great deal in the way of flora and fauna. Each hole is quite separate, so that after a little while one feels one is playing golf inside a kind of cocoon."

Gleneagles Hotel has played host to major golf tournaments from its beginning.

The event with the longest association is, of course, The Silver Tassie. The trophy itself was presented in 1925 by the L.M.S. Railway Company for a competition intended to rank with the Royal St George's Challenge Cup and Gold Vase. It took its name from what was then the second hole on the King's course, and was in the form of a silver quaich—a Scottish drinking cup.

The first tournament was held on 12th September, 1925, with more than a hundred golfers competing over the two courses. The winner was Cyril Tolley, who equalled the amateur record for King's with a 71, and created a new record for the extended Queen's with a 70.

(The Silver Tassie after almost 40 years as one of Scotland's most popular golfing events, lapsed in the 1960s, but in 1982 was revived again in a new format. It is now a foursomes competition on a knock-out basis, and its future as an annual event seems assured).

After the Second World War, in 1948, the Penfold Tournament was won by James Adams, and in the Fifties came the Gleneagles Saxone Tournament—a Pro-Am event and possibly the first of its kind to be held anywhere. A Gleneagles Tournament was also held, and this continued into the Sixties. A Dunlop Tournament took place in 1960.

The 13th tee at King's, 'Braid's Brawest'. One of the world's greatest par 4 holes.

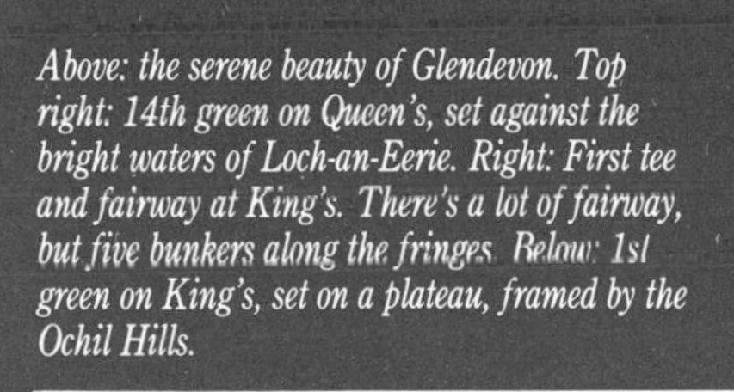

Above: the serene beauty of Glendevon. Top right: 14th green on Queen's, set against the bright waters of Loch-an-Eerie. Right: First tee and fairway at King's. There's a lot of fairway, but five bunkers along the fringes. Below: 1st green on King's, set on a plateau, framed by the Ochil Hills.

More ambitiously, the Double Diamond Tournament of 1974, '76 and '77 featured teams from the United States, Australasia and the Continent of Europe.

It was in 1975 that Gleneagles golf was brought to the notice of a universal audience through a BBC 2 Television programme screened under the title Pro-Celebrity Golf. The idea behind it was entirely new: the teaming up of famous professional golfers with personalities equally famous in the entertainment world and then letting them loose on an historic Scottish golf course.

Both parties converged on Gleneagles with pleasurable anticipation of a week's stay in a palatial hotel—and daily golf in front of the cameras.

That first year the celebrities included Bing Crosby and Howard Keel from the United States, Dickie Henderson and Charlie Drake from the United Kingdom, and the racing driver James Hunt.

The programme content of fascinating professional skill and sheer entertainment value (as when Telly Savalas worked his way round the course shouting "I love ya baby!" at every opportunity) attracted a delighted family audience of four million.

In 1976 professionals Johnny Miller and Tony Jacklin starred with, among others, Sean Connery, Val Doonican and Jackie Stewart. Burt Lancaster and Alan Shepard, the astronaut, also put in an appearance. On fine days, in brilliant sunshine under a summer sky, the most glamorous star of the show was The Gleneagles Hotel itself.

Tom Watson and Greg Norman, who have made an appearance at the pro-celeb tournaments.

Names and faces who helped make Gleneagles Hotel synonymous with pro-celebrity golf. Top left: Bing Crosby and Val Doonican. Above: Crosby and Sean Connery. Left: Jackie Stewart, Crosby, Connery and Phil Harris. Below: Charlie Drake, and former hotel general manager, Guy Macpherson with Telly Savalas, famous for doing his well-known 'Who loves ya, baby?' all around the Course.

The Pro-Celebrity films have since been distributed round the world, and the event is now established as one of the firmest of sporting television favourites.

If the emphasis on difficult, exclusive, celebrity golf at times seems to take precedence, and even become a little intimidating, this is certainly not the Gleneagles norm. Gleneagles is for everybody, as the company's multilateral thinking bears out. It has been established that only a small proportion of hotel guests play golf at all—in fact, about 20 per cent—and of those a still smaller number are professional or famous. Everyone else has at his or her disposal some of the finest inland golf courses in Britain.

Ian Marchbank succinctly confirms the situation: "Courses are for golfers, not just championships. I never want to learn that one of our guests has come here and played one of our courses with his wife, and then gone away saying 'We've never been so miserable on a golf course in our lives!'

"The fact is everyone can enjoy golf at Gleneagles whether they are beginners or professionals."

Peter Alliss, king of golf commentators, summed it up nicely when he once remarked: "On a fine day at Gleneagles Hotel, who could wish for anything more?"

Peter Alliss, king of the golf commentators.

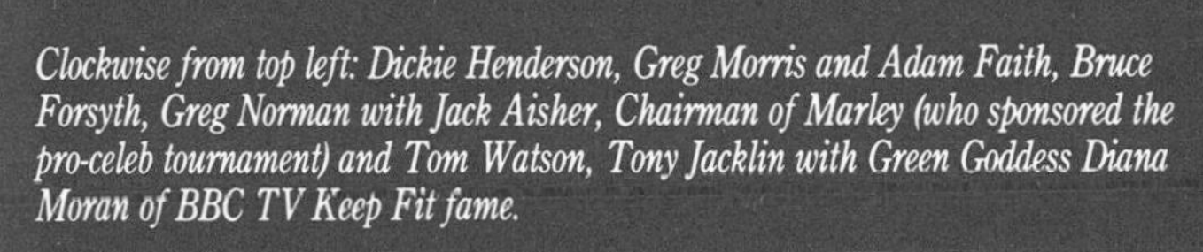

Clockwise from top left: Dickie Henderson, Greg Morris and Adam Faith, Bruce Forsyth, Greg Norman with Jack Aisher, Chairman of Marley (who sponsored the pro-celeb tournament) and Tom Watson, Tony Jacklin with Green Goddess Diana Moran of BBC TV Keep Fit fame.

From left: Jimmy Tarbuck and Mrs. Tarbuck, Tom Watson, Sean and Mrs. Connery, Mrs. Watson and Greg Norman.

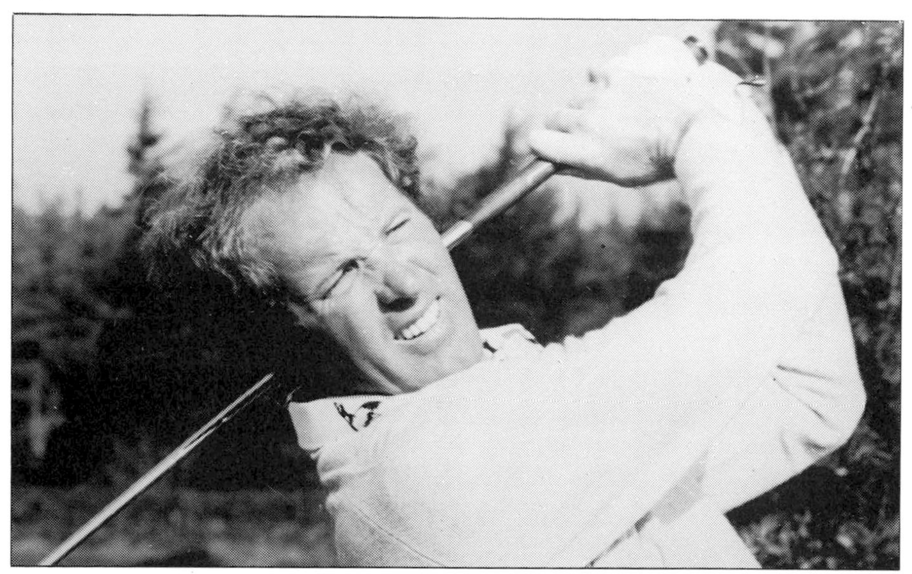

One of the pro's, and no less a celebrity, Tom Weiskopf.

From left: Partners Weiskopf with American comedian Dick Martin; Bruce Forsyth with Peter Oosterhuis.

100 LG

INTO THE 21ST CENTURY

"GLENEAGLES IS NO LONGER TO BE JUST FOR PEOPLE WHO WANT TO PLAY GOLF AND STAY IN HOTELS... WE WANT TO APPEAL ON A MUCH BROADER BASIS."

GLENEAGLES HOTEL is known locally as The Big House, and for The Big House, as for everywhere else, the Second World War changed everything. It emerged from its role as a military hospital and miners' rehabilitation centre with few reminders of its former glamour. The gilt had gone from the name, and a Herculean task faced the executives of the L.M.S. in 1947, and those of British Transport Hotels who took over when the railways were nationalised in 1948.

Despite shortages of everything the interior was refurbished and the high living began again – although the fifties were to reveal that the traditional Gleneagles clientele – Donald Matheson's "travelling class" – were changing in habit and taste and no longer inclined to drive their limousines up to the front door in anything like the same numbers.

Nevertheless, quite a few of the well-known regulars continued to appear – notably Lady Gamage, a charismatic guest of the pre-war years. Then there was "The Pineapple King", an old millionaire from Hawaii, who used to carry a roll of £5 notes and hand out one every time he felt like giving a tip.

The Maharajah of Bhopal did arrive for the grouse season in a special train with a party of eighteen, including security men, three cooks and his chauffeur. He took twelve rooms for five weeks. At today's prices, he spent more than £12,000.

A New York stockbroker booked in with his wife, three children and a nanny and stayed for a month. His bill came to £3,300.

Another American millionaire thought he would like to fish on the River Earn – knowing nothing about a sport which often takes the form of a fine art. To the astonishment of everyone – not least his ghillie – he grassed an 18lb salmon. The proud angler celebrated by throwing a cocktail party for every guest in the hotel. The fish lay in state on a catafalque of heather. Next day it was preserved for ever by a taxidermist, suitably framed and flown to the United States.

In 1971 Gleneagles Hotel played host to 150 members of the Chief Executives Forum of the United States, and their wives. Every man was a dollar millionaire and the party spent £6,000 a day for five days, highlighting their visit with the attendance of pipers and Scottish country dancers and a spectacular firework display.

Work on the Gleneagles Hotel of the future began in 1981, which included a refurbished lounge bar. With the addition of the new leisure complex, the hotel became a year-round resort.

The Ballroom

In 1977 the British Government entertained thirty-five Commonwealth leaders and their wives. The bill for their weekend of deliberation and recreation came to £50,000, but out of the meeting came the often-quoted Gleneagles Agreement with reference to racism in sport.

The Defence Ministers of N.A.T.O. conferred at the hotel in 1981—a high-powered occasion during which the building was sealed off, all flying in the area was forbidden, and to the amusement of all concerned, even Ginger, the hotel cat who spends much of his time asleep on a chair in the entrance hall, was issued with his own security pass.

In 1981, when the long-term fate of Gleneagles Hotel as an enterprise hung in the balance, salvation came in the shape of a new company formed to buy three of Scotland's most famous railway hotels under a government privatisation scheme: the Caledonian and North British in Edinburgh—and Gleneagles. Where Gleneagles was concerned, their arrival was just in time.

The company took the name of Gleneagles Hotels plc, its executives were described as "young, commercial, entrepreneurial and aggressive," and plans were announced for the essential and very welcome spending at Gleneagles of more than £5 million over the next three years.

"Gleneagles is no longer to be just for people who want to play golf and stay in hotels," the Press were told. "We want to appeal on a much broader basis and cater for a far wider market."

Peter Tyrie, the managing director with extensive international experience, first saw the hotel in the sixties, and then again as one of the inheritors in 1981.

"I was, of course, very saddened to see the lack of investment at Gleneagles due to cash restraints from the railways who were divesting their hotel interests. Gleneagles Hotel is unique in the world—there is nowhere to equal the majesty of that property—and it is up to us to develop its potential to the fullest and at the same time retain the character and beauty we have inherited. Our business is also about people and service, and in that we are backed by a long tradition of Scottish hospitality."

Most impressive of all was the new company's intention to keep the hotel open all the year round—for the first time since 1926—and construct a £1.5 million leisure complex for use by guests and members of a new Country Club.

In the autumn of 1981 The Big House was closed and became a ghostly relic of its former self. London designers and their contractors moved into the shrouded lounges and silent corridors and began the task of restoring the hotel to its former grandeur and gracefully leading it into the 21st century.

The work ranged from essential repairs to the enormous roof to the addition of bedrooms, the rebuilding of the cocktail bar and the installation of £40,000 worth of new equipment in the kitchens. The exterior paintwork was renewed, over a thousand sash cords were fitted to windows, ground floor areas were double glazed, open fires were introduced into the main lounge which had also undergone splendid redecoration in cream, gold and red. The crowning innovation was the leisure centre housed under a huge glass dome close to the main building.

A covered glass walkway leads through a Japanese garden floodlit at night and equipped with a barbecue pit for summer events. Inside the dome there is an abrupt change of both climate and scenery—from the

The new glass-covered walkway to the swimming pool and leisure complex area. At right and below: the auctions at the hotel by Sotheby's, which include sales not only of golf equipment, but fine art and furniture.

often bracing Moor of Auchterarder to the steady 78 degrees of a sub-tropical paradise furnished with a large swimming pool, a jacuzzi, sauna, solariums, massage, squash courts, snooker tables and table tennis.

A terrace with tables and sun umbrellas adjoins a self-service buffet, brasserie and bar. There is a dance floor for evening discotheques. Although the project was undertaken mainly to provide extra recreation for hotel guests, there is also a Country Club clientele whose members pay an annual fee.

More than any other asset, this exotic facility brings Gleneagles Hotel closer to the status planned for it—that of "the complete resort." In recent years visits by families were on the decline, but the Country Club has brought them back in large numbers. As for the business community, a company director enquiring about accommodation for his conference is not only impressed by the hotel but by the leisure complex and all it has to offer.

In November, 1982, Gleneagles Hotel came into its own again at a gala weekend which made headlines recalling those of the twenties. Limousines queued once more at the door. Royal Silversmiths and International Jewellers, Mappin & Webb flew in £5 million of the latest French jewellery from their branches in Paris and Cannes. Rolls-Royce sent a display of its finest cars and Louis Feraud in conjunction with Mappin & Webb put on a fashion show featuring £20,000 dresses and millions of pounds worth of jewellery.

The imagination and energy applied to refurbishing the fabric was meanwhile being matched in equal measure in the kitchens and dining rooms.

Barry Aspinall, Food and Beverage manager, came to Gleneagles from Canada after five years in North America.

"When I first came here I expected a Scottish culinary experience—but I was handed a French menu! On it were items which have been routine in large hotels for the past hundred years—totally predictable. So we conducted a search throughout the world for a new taste: A Taste of Canada, a Taste of New Zealand, a Taste of Scotland. Scottish cuisine is quite heavy in character, but it can be very well done, particularly as we have here some of the finest natural produce in the world—salmon, beef, game, shellfish, vegetables, fruit. From all this we've created our own cuisine, which we call A Taste of Gleneagles.

The swimming pool area features jacuzzi, lounge and snack bar with barbecue.

A gala weekend in 1982 evoked memories of the Roaring Twenties. Rolls Royce sent a display of its finest, including this 1907 Silver Ghost — insured for a £1 million. Mappin & Webb displayed £5 million worth of jewellery and Louis Ferraud put on a fashion show featuring £20,000 dresses.

"Normally the creation of a hotel menu involves two people—the chef and the food and beverage manager—who present it to the general manager, and he approves it. At Gleneagles we've tried something very different. We assembled all the chefs in our Kitchen Brigade, with their various skills and experience from elsewhere. We suggested the types of dishes and asked them to return in three weeks with what they had created.

"This they did. The dishes were all good, imaginative, individual, and we chose the best. Some had to be made less elaborate—bearing in mind that sometimes we're called upon to serve four hundred meals..."

From then on the menu for the Strathearn Restaurant included soup flavoured with venison and hare and juniper berries; trout and pheasant smoked in the kitchens; Aberdeen Angus fillet steak with lobster tail in lemon butter; fresh venison with poached pear and redcurrant sauce; layers of River Tay salmon baked in butter pastry.

At the back of the menu appeared the names of some forty chefs concerned in its creation—suggesting a specific personal interest and involvement in what the guests were eating.

The general manager appointed at this time of transformation was Guy Grant Macpherson, who had previously spent three years as general manager of the famous resort hotel of Sandy Lane, in Barbados. Sitting in the lounge at the beginning of his second winter season he cast a professional eye over a flurry of arrivals in the entrance hall.

"All the work has been very worth while, and we are now finding the much wider market we were looking for. We're becoming quite used to seeing the chairmen of companies and show business personalities landing on the lawn by helicopter, but at the same time we have Country Club members arriving to spend the day and a lot of golfers on two or three night packages. Then, Sundays are particularly successful. Family Sunday lunch was a dying tradition here—we once only did about thirty—but now we have Sunday *brunch*, with an out-of-this-world buffet and a Dixieland jazz band. Families love it and we often serve three hundred meals."

Guy Macpherson has now taken up another appointment, but during his time at Gleneagles he was especially complimentary about his staff, whom he described as predominantly Scottish, young, enthusiastic and friendly, and with a genuine liking for the place. (The hotel plays an important role in the training of staff to five-star standards—an opportunity not easily obtainable outside London.)

Gleneagles Hotel has long been favoured as a conference centre. In recognition of this a new conference suite has been provided—equipped with every modern aid including facilities for simultaneous translations. The maximum capacity is four hundred, but the area is divisible into three sections. As very large business gatherings tend to overwhelm the daily life of the hotel, the aim is rather to encourage the demand for select conferences of up to fifty people—and this is already being attracted.

Tennis at Gleneagles Hotel has made news since the early beginnings, though never so prominently as golf. The existing hard courts have been re-surfaced, and the company is now paying more than passing attention to the further promotion of tennis, even envisaging Gleneagles as the future tennis centre of Scotland—something which has always been lacking.

Virginia Wade, the international tennis star, expressed her own pleasure at becoming touring professional at the hotel in 1983: "I was brought up

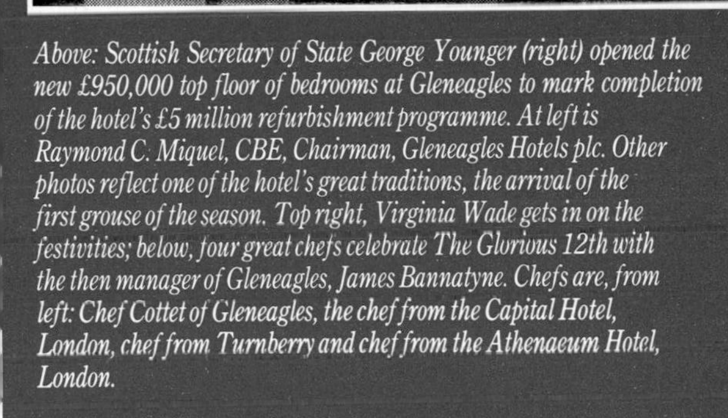

Above: Scottish Secretary of State George Younger (right) opened the new £950,000 top floor of bedrooms at Gleneagles to mark completion of the hotel's £5 million refurbishment programme. At left is Raymond C. Miquel, CBE, Chairman, Gleneagles Hotels plc. Other photos reflect one of the hotel's great traditions, the arrival of the first grouse of the season. Top right, Virginia Wade gets in on the festivities; below, four great chefs celebrate The Glorious 12th with the then manager of Gleneagles, James Bannatyne. Chefs are, from left: Chef Cottet of Gleneagles, the chef from the Capital Hotel, London, chef from Turnberry and chef from the Athenaeum Hotel, London.

with a Scottish background and I've been to Scotland many times and am crazy about it. I really go for the atmosphere here."

The Managing Director of the Gleneagles Hotels, Peter Tyrie, says: "We should like eventually to have tennis as closely associated with the hotel as golf has been, and we are certainly considering how to develop it here into an indoor spectator sport."

The company's intentions where Gleneagles golf is concerned are equally reassuring. "Our attitude towards our golf is only that in the years to come it must continue to be the best, and plans are afoot to build a fifth course sometime before 1990—to be established as a championship venue of an individual and different character. It will contrive to uplift the level of play still more—no doubt it will become *very* select— and thus will add to our already international reputation."

It is typical of Gleneagles in the 1980s that while work continued through its second winter season with the re-decoration of over a hundred rooms and the addition of more guest bedrooms, management and staff were finalising plans for a huge and spectacular party for their Christmas guests.

In February 1984, a further stride into the 21st century took place when Gleneagles Hotels plc was acquired by Arthur Bell & Sons plc, the independent legendary Whisky Distillers—a marriage of two great Scottish institutions which augers well for the century to come. Raymond Miquel, CBE, Chairman of Bell's, became Chairman of Gleneagles Hotels.

General Manager, James Bannatyne who was awarded the MBE in 1980, photographed with his staff to mark the occasion.

I REMEMBER GLENEAGLES HOTEL...

IN RESPONSE TO AN APPEAL FOR REMINISCENCES OF GLENEAGLES HOTEL IN THE EARLIER DAYS OF ITS HISTORY, FORMER GUESTS AND MEMBERS OF THE STAFF HAVE JOINED FORCES TO FURNISH A FINAL CHAPTER, OFFERING VIVID PERSONAL IMPRESSIONS OF GLENEAGLES AT VARIOUS STAGES OF ITS EXCLUSIVE AND COLOURFUL HISTORY.

SPACE IS NOT AVAILABLE FOR THEM ALL, BUT THOSE REPRODUCED HERE ARE SUITABLY REPRESENTATIVE OF THE PASSING YEARS, AND WILL INVOKE MANY A MEMORY FOR THOSE WHO AT ANY TIME HAVE KNOWN AND LOVED THE HOTEL FOR THE GRAND AND UNIQUE INSTITUTION IT IS.

SCOTLAND'S ONLY HOTEL BANK

In 1924 I was clerk in the Auchterarder office of the old Union Bank of Scotland, and it was the Agent (manager) there who arranged for a sub-office to be opened inside the hotel. I like to think we were pioneers in this respect. We were provided with a small room and we opened for business before all the furnishings were installed.

Our first customer was a dishy young lady from the United States who cashed some American Express cheques. If you will believe me, her name was Belle Presse.

My work was to shuttle between Auchterarder and the hotel, on my push-bike, carrying the cash book, correspondence, and change—quite a bag at times. My daily journeys (including Saturdays, of course) could be extremely awkward, battling with the heavy bag against all kinds of weather.

The hotel cashiers and the various departments lodged their takings every day and we did the necessary accounting required. Very large sums passed through our little office, and I question very much if modern staffs would care to run the risks we ran in transporting cash on a push-bike, without any kind of escort. Yet we never thought anything of it at the time.

We had occasional glimpses of visiting celebrities: a spare figure in Norfolk jacket and knickerbockers was pointed out to me as George Bernard Shaw, and I wished he had come in to cash a cheque. A very smart and attractive young lady was Peggy O'Neill, a pin-up girl of the day.

On Thursdays we paid out the wages to the staff. It was an education meeting them—the bustling porters, the impudent page boys, the amiable chamber maids, the polite waiters and the strange chaps who emerged from the depths of the kitchen, and other men and girls moving in their own orbits within the general organisation of the hotel.

At the end of the season the staff began to be transferred away to other hotels, and it was sad saying good-bye to some of them. One was a waiter who had served in the train dining-cars. He told me how he had once been summoned by an irate lady, the wife of some high official of the L.M.S., who ticked him off about the wine he had served and demanded to know where he had got the stuff.

"From the company's cellars, ma'am," he replied.—GEORGE M. MALTMAN, Dorset.

A COUNTY ASSEMBLAGE

Over 500 dancers foregathered in the beautiful ivory and gold ballroom of the hotel after dinner had been served in the magnificently appointed dining hall, and with many representatives of county families present, the assemblage was a brilliant one. Giant crystal candelabra lit up the scene with wonderful effect, the mirrored wall reflecting again the splendid moving pageant of feminine fashion, contrasting with the sober evening garb and the kilted dress of the male dancers. Entrancing music was discoursed by Gleneagles Hotel Orchestra.

Hon. Mrs Stirling was wearing an elegant gown of parma georgette, the batteau neck outlined in diamente and encrustations of diamente enhanced the veiled skirt. With diamond and pearl earrings she wore thrice-looped pearls...

The Duke of Atholl accompanied a large party, in which was Mrs Harrison Wallace, whose gown of turquoise blue ninon veiled silver tissue clasped to one shoulder by a cluster of blue. To correspond were draperies in ombre ninon, which fell to the hem at the back. Round her throat were lovely pearls, and in her hair she wore a diamond ornament. Mrs L. G. Harrison chose black georgette draped over satin, and from the ceinture of gold were appliquéd motifs in front. Miss McCallum affected dawn pink chiffon with swathed sash and waterfall flounces...—Report in *THE DUNDEE COURIER AND ADVERTISER*, 1926.

BRIGHT YOUNG THINGS

I was present at the dinner dance on the night that Henry Hall made the first broadcast from the hotel. We had a large party of "Bright Young Things" and when the time came for the band to go on the air we were making rather a racket, and sitting quite close to the bandstand. Eventually a waiter arrived to ask us if we could "pipe down"—as the rather primitive mike was picking *us* up instead of Henry Hall! We were forgiven, of course.

After a good many years—in 1947, I think—my husband nearly expired when he was asked to pay 30s each for champagne cocktails in the American Bar!—Mrs E. M. DRISCOLL, Wokingham, Berkshire.

A BALLROOM TO OURSELVES

My wife and I stayed at Gleneagles Hotel on the nights of 4th and 5th June, 1926, at the start of our honeymoon. Henry Hall and his band were in the ballroom and we had his music and the whole of the room to ourselves. Our apartments—the height of luxury—cost £1 10s per night. Breakfast was 4s 6d each. Lunch 6s, dinner 8s 6d per person. Half a bottle of wine was 2s 6d. Aerated water, 1s.

The total number of residents was, I think, about ten. In the garage were three Rolls-Royces and one snub-nosed Morris, which was ours. It was of great interest to the chauffeurs!

At this time there was, of course, the General Strike.—WILLIAM READ, Harrogate.

G.B. Shaw was a regular, in Norfolk jacket and knickerbockers. Many remember dancing in the ballroom to the music of Henry Hall. Among exhibition ballroom dancers in the 1920's were Josephine Bradley and Wellesley Smith (above right) who also enjoyed the golf.

HENRY HALL REMEMBERS

Henry Hall, now 86 retired to Eastbourne, kindly sent us his own brief reminiscence of opening night at Gleneagles Hotel.

"I remember the excitement of the evening on that June night in 1924. They had just finished the final decorations of the ballroom. The microphone and the transmitter to be used for broadcasting were all new things for me. Hopes were high in the band—we were going to be transmitted on a nationwide programme!

A right royal reception was organised and on the occasion a new face was being introduced to broadcasting—me!"

Henry Hall
Eastbourne

CHANGED DAYS

In about 1927, as a young man of about nineteen, I was travelling with a certain Major Turner who was my tutor at the time, when his car broke down in the early evening not far from the hotel. He decided that we would stay the night there while it was being repaired. It was the close season and the hotel was practically empty. After dinner a bank manager from Auchterarder came in for a drink with his very pretty young daughter. The Major knew the father, and while they were having a drink together I asked the girl if she would like to dance. We went into the ballroom where Henry Hall was conducting the band. The only other people in the room were two professional dance partners dancing together. My young friend and I proceeded to dance, but were politely asked not to.

Why?

I was not wearing evening dress!—(The Rev.) GEORGE MACKENZIE, Pulborough, West Sussex.

CHILDHOOD RECOLLECTIONS

I was brought up in Auchterarder.

While the hotel was standing only half built at the end of the First War it was regarded in the village as "a White Elephant". I remember hearing that expression for the first time as a child, when I over heard a conversation amongst some locals. When the hotel opened a lot of local lads and lassies found work as cleaners and day maids.

The L.M.S. staff who were married took rooms in the village and brought their families—most were French or Italian and married to English girls. The father and uncle of Adrienne Corrie (the actress)—Luigi Riccaboni and brother—worked as chefs or waiters. Adrienne was then in a pram.

Henry Hall's band played at teatime, and as a teenager I used to walk up to the hotel on a Sunday with friends and swim and enjoy tea and the dance tunes for the sum of 2s 6d. Jimmy Leach and several other bandsmen lodged in Auchterarder. They were rather splendid in their white blazers.

The ponds in the hotel grounds were a godsend in winter, when we used to skate on them. Wrapped in scarves and tammies we greatly enjoyed ourselves.

Some of the regular visitors were known to the locals by reputation. There was "The Pineapple King", renowned for his amazing generosity. There was "The Prince of Nepal". (Knowing th Nepalese later in life I presume this was one of th Rana family.) The Prince of Wales came for gol Bobby Jones and Max Falkener were regulars a competitions—Max always very gaily dressed i plus fours and yellow stockings.

In the early days a number of "worthies returned to the hotel each season. One of th caddies was known as Coocoo (cuckoo). Everyon became aware of his return as he coocoo-ed hi way from the course to his favourite pub i Auchterarder.

"The Coocoo's arrived!" was a greetin amongst all his cronies.

On one occasion a local bigwig wrote to th Press that he had heard the cuckoo on a certai date which he claimed was a record. A length correspondence ensued, he insisting that he' heard the bird *distinctly* at a certain time. He wa somewhat deflated when it was eventually dis closed that his "cuckoo" had been caddying a Gleneagles Hotel!—ANNE HALDANE LONGLE (née McLaughlan), East Preston, West Sussex.

WINDFALL ON THE FAIRWAY

"A young Irish caddie who carries th sticks round the Queen's course a Gleneagles Hotel, has had a lucky find whic makes him the richer by £250.

Over a year ago the loss of a fine pearl valued a that sum, was reported to the police as havin been lost in the vicinity of the third hole. Th woman who reported the loss went abroad an when the caddy found the pearl efforts to trac her failed.

The statutory period during which lost propert is retained for restoration having expired, th caddy has now fallen heir to the jewel."—NEWS ITEM, *Glasgow Evening Times*, 29th May, 1927.

DARING THEFT AT GLENEAGLES

A theft of jewellery from Gleneagles Hotel has been reported to the Perthshire police uthorities. The missing property is understood o be of the value of about £1500.

It appears that the jewels, which belonged to a dy temporarily residing at the hotel, were stolen om a jewel case in her bedroom.

In all, eight articles of jewellery were stolen—a aluable diamond and platinum bracelet, a iamond and sapphire brooch, four rings and two vatches.

When the lady discovered her loss all members f the staff were immediately interviewed, but no ne was able to shed any light on the mystery. The thief, whoever he was, executed the robbery n a skilful and swift manner, as none of the ervants or patrons of the hotel saw anyone ntering the room.

In a short time the police arrived and nvestigated the scene of the robbery. Extensive search was made for fingerprints and other clues which the intruder may have left in the bed-oom.

It is understood that the district is being watched for a suspected man.—NEWS ITEM, *Glasgow Evening News,* 9th January, 1928.

PERFECT SILHOUETTES

"As you wander becarpeted from sun-lounge to dining hall, from smoke room and drawing room, billiards room, writing room, and every other kind of room to ballroom and swimming pool, your senses are charmed by almost every decorative mood from French grey and Rose du Barri to pastel blue and old gold and sunshine yellow; great Ionic pillars and pilasters rise before you; through every stately window you see always the Perthshire hills strong and subtle with all the unbelievable colour in which D.Y. Cameron steeps his hillscapes.

Against such a background move your people: people of charm and discretion, people whose talk in the lounges is as vivacious as a flight of seagulls or swifts in the sunlight; young British girls with the perfect tennis and golf silhouette, American girls with a gusty impetuosity about them, plus-four and Fair Isle pullover men as to the manner born.

With clubs and racquets they go jauntily out to an atmosphere transparent as a newly washed pane of glass, and breathe an air with the wine of the heather and milk of the gorse in it. They go over lawns and past flower beds crimson with dahlias and through thickets of shrubs and rowan trees, and so to a billowy wilderness of broom, heather and gorse where the secret greens of the King's and Queen's links stretch like a chain of emeralds from hills to hills; or they go to the *en tout cas* courts sunk from the wind between the brightness of herbaceous borders.—TREVOR ALLEN in *The Westminster Gazette*, 1926.

£1,500 GEMS VANISH.

Gleneagles Hotel Mystery.

LADY'S LOSS

Mysterious events at Gleneagles Hotel made news, a la Agatha Christie.

The Prince of Wales, as he was then (later Edward VIII who abdicated) talking to the Duchess of Portland, in a photo taken in the late 1920's.

A Sociable Social Secretary

In April, 1925, I replied to an advertisement in *The Daily Telegraph* for an assistant sports secretary at "a Scottish hotel." I was interviewed at the L.M.S.R's St Pancras Hotel by Gordon Yates—then Comptroller of Entertainments—with Mrs Muggeridge, who was Sir Francis Towle's sister and a very formidable lady!

When Gordon Yates revealed that the hotel was Gleneagles, advertised so extensively as "The Mecca of Sport", I was absolutely intrigued. My duties would be as assistant-secretary to Major J.C.S. Rendall, then the resident tennis professional and also, I believe, the Hard Courts Pro. of Europe. I would have nine lovely *en tout* courts under my charge, a groundsman and six ball-boys. On wet days I would have to organise amusements inside the hotel—treasure hunts, badminton, and so on.

I got the job.

When I started my duties ten days later the hotel had been open for a year. The manager was Frank Fisher—a young, rather Cockney type of man in his late twenties—and assistant manager was Victor Lomax, a cousin of the Towles.

This was the height of the Charleston era and I was very keen on dancing. Before long, apart from my sports activities, I found myself deputising as hostess in the ballroom. I loved every minute. I heard Henry Hall do his first broadcast—we were all asked to cluster round the microphone and clap.

In the quiet season we danced in the Sun Room, with its charming half-moon shape and wonderful long bright yellow curtains and notes of music printed round the pelmets. Evenings were livelier on Wednesdays and Saturdays, when the dancing in the ballroom was attended by the R.A.F. from Leuchars, the Royal Navy from Rosyth, the Black Watch from Perth and the Argylle and Sutherland Highlanders from Stirling. There was frequently a dearth of lady partners—in those days everybody waited to be introduced!

When the season became busier, from the end of June, we used to have professional dancing couples for a fortnight at a time: Joyce Bradley and her partner, Phyllis Haylor and Eric Miller—all world champions of their time. These dancers gave demonstrations and could be booked for private dancing lessons.

The summer of 1925 was perfect, in June it seemed never to get dark. I shall always remember the golden broom on the golf course, and the men so sun-tanned—they all looked incredibly handsome!

By contrast, 1926 was miserably wet. I used to spend sleepless nights wondering how I was going to organise something amusing for the younger guests.

Among those many distinguished people who came to stay I remember very well the Berry family (Proprietors of *The Daily Telegraph*).There were three teenage sons who were wonderful allies of mine—they preferred to help organise rather than take part.

Many well-known Americans included Severin Bourne, the heir to Singer Sewing Machines, with his wife and family. The young daughter Barbara was a special friend of mine.

I also came to know many of the local families—the Pullars of Perth, the Muirs of Braco, the Falconer-Stewarts, who had two children named Hansel and Gretel and lived in a local castle.

There were, of course, memorable personalities amongst the staff, notably Hughie Catterall (hall porter), Josef the head waiter, and Gavardi, the head of the grill room.

Returning to the guests, I do remember a Mr Colgate asking me what toothpaste I used. I didn't know at the time who he was—and I fear I did not give him the answer he hoped for!—(Mrs) Doris Heath (née Monk), New Milton, Hants.

An Italian Connection

My mother, whose maiden name was May Brown, and her two sisters Agnes and Bella, were three of nine children born in Liverpool. They were all working in the Adelphi Hotel in Liverpool when, to my grandmother's mild consternation each brought home an Italian boy-friend and proceeded to marry him. My mother and Agnes were chosen to join staff of the brand new Gleneagles Hotel in the year that it opened—1924. She was eighteen at the time and very excited about it—but on arrival the place was to her, of course, completely out in the wilds. Auchterarder seemed no more than a few cottages, a couple of churches and a pub.

According to my mother, she spent the first three days weeping—she was so very homesick for Liverpool. Mr Turnbull, who was then in charge, said: "For goodness sake, May, you don't realise what an honour it is to be sent here. This hotel is going to be on the map for all time!".

Meanwhile the decorators were in and the marvellous carpets were being unpacked, and everyone became very busy.

Eventually my mother returned to Liverpool and it was Aunt Agnes who stayed on. Hers was the first Gleneagles Hotel romance. She met Victor Barberis. They were married in Glasgow and went straight on duty in the hotel the next morning.

Little did my mother know that on returning to Liverpool she was to meet Louie Prada, and marry him. She produced my elder brother Louie, and then me, and after that we were all dispatche[d] back to the Gleneagles Hotel.

On the first night my parents were invited t[o] have dinner with the head chef—a fantasti[c] honour. My brother and I were left in a twin bedded room. I heard music and wandered downstairs in my little wincyette nightie. I wa[s] apparently having a lovely time being waltze[d] round the floor until a telephone was used to as[k] my parents if they would mind retrieving the[ir] daughter.

They were terribly embarrassed to find me in the company of a distinguished lady in a fantasti[c] backless gown, playing with her necklace, bu[t] everyone was very kind about it.

Aldo Sebilia, my other uncle, was always sent to open the du Soleil Room, which was used for the shooting season. His wage was ten shillings a week, so he relied heavily on his tips. These were usually generous. As a naturalised British Subject, Uncle Aldo went to war in 1939. He was sent to the Far East and ended as a Japanese Prisoner of War working on the Burma Railway where he died.

At Gleneagles he had a very fine voice and was often asked to sing. He was known as "The Singing Waiter of the du Soleil."

My father had a hotel story about the various fruits which were served untouched by human hand. When he peeled peaches, oranges and apples for guests like Sir Barry Jackson, the peel was taken off all in one piece. He was a great artist in this. All the game was pressed at the table and the juice served on the spot. Gleneagles Hotel service was of the very highest order.

One of my mother's fondest memories is of walking in the hotel grounds one afternoon in the thirties and coming across a lady painting or sketching. She told my mother what lovely hands her daughter had, and proceeded to make sketches of my baby hands. Later, my mother learned that the artist was Dame Laura Knight, and I often wonder if she ever used those sketches in any of her subsequent portraits.

For us, one of the most tragic happenings of the Second War was the sinking of the merchant ship *Arandora Star* in June, 1940. It was taking non-naturalised Italians and Germans—mostly catering staff—to Canada. Although the boat was sailing under the Red Cross, most of the occupants were locked in cabins and there was a lot of barbed wire on deck.

When it got out of the Mersey it was torpedoed by a U-boat. The people in it didn't have a lot of chance of getting out. This was actually one of the reasons why after the war there was such a shortage of chefs and waiters—part of a whole generation of expert catering staff was lost. My own father lost so many friends in one night.

My mother, who was eighteen when she joined the first staff of Gleneagles Hotel in 1924, is now in her eighties. Although she wept for the first three days she now likes to recall that her happiest times were in Scotland, and she ended up by loving it and wishing she had never left it.—(Mrs.) Yolanda Ottonello, Strathmore Hotel, Morecambe, Lancashire.

GLENEAGLES HOTEL,
PERTHSHIRE.

EACE ANNIVERSARY
ALA DINNER DANCE

Saturday, November 13th, 1926.

Inclusive charge, 10/6

Book your tables now.

Arthur Towle, Controller.

GLENEAGLES
HOTEL

Perthshire
Scotland

For Christmas
and New Year

"Britain's Greatest Reso
Hotel"

OUTDOOR SPORTS
BRILLIANT GALAS
JOYOUS FESTIVITIES

Reserve Accommodation No
Apply Resident Manager

RTHUR TOWLE Controller L.M.S. HOTELS

Some of the Professionals

GORDON LOCKHART
Gleneagles

Gleneagles Hotel was where Society went to be seen and to be written about in the press and in The Tatler. Charity balls and galas were all the rage then. Golf of course was a prime attraction and Gordon Lockhart, the hotel's first 'golf pro' even took time out to take a girl skater in hand on one of the course's frozen lochs.

NO ALTO SAXOPHONE!

As a family we stayed in the hotel almost up to the outbreak of war. I well recall the dramatic days when the war had become unavoidable. The recall of Parliament seemed to involve about half the guests, and the whole company assembled in the lounge to listen to the Prime Minister and Foreign Secretary on a primitive wireless set, with their forecast of doom.

My main impression of Gleneagles as a hotel is that it was the one and only place that suited the whole family. My father and I were keen on golf, my mother enjoyed the comfort and service, and my brother all of these, plus the presence of girls! I met my own wife there in 1953.

Among the regular visitors in the seasons before (and after) the war were the Cowan Dobsons—a painter of renown and his wife—and often his glamourous model. He was a member of the Magic Circle—an expert conjurer who could be persuaded to perform for a small group remarkable card tricks.

Henry Hall's successor in charge of music at Gleneagles was Joe Orlando, director of music for the L.M.S. Hotels. I knew him as a courteous, well-groomed band leader, whose appearance at Gleneagles was more in the nature of inspecting his troops. He would, however, play in the band in an inconspicuous position.

His signature tune, which at midnight sadly brought the evening dancing to a close, was *I'll See You in my Dreams,* as played by every Orlando band. (The bands, incidentally, had a characteristic sound, due in part to a L.M.S. director's refusal to countenance the use of the alto saxophone.)—J. A. COLVER, Sheffield.

THE HOTEL AS HOSPITAL

My time at Gleneagles started on 25th January, 1943. I remember walking up the approach road from the posh little station on a bright frosty afternoon with snow on the grass verges. I even remember what I was wearing, because it was wartime and coupons were short, and I had had the good luck to be given a coat-length of tweed, which I had just made up, with hat to match. I was getting away from a boring job in London, tired of not finding a decent place to live, and the long journeys to work.

I had applied for a job with the Department of Health for Scotland as a physiotherapist, and was offered a post at Gleneagles. The hotel had been a military hospital and was now changing over to a Fitness Centre for Scottish Miners.

All kinds of adaptations had been made. The public rooms on the ground floor were fitted out as gymnasiums and occupational and physiotherapy departments.

My gymnasium was the immense front lounge. The walls were fitted with wall-bars and exercise apparatus; the pillars were protected with mattresses and the ceiling light fittings encased in wire cages. The room was so big that for my first week my voice was strained—until I learned how to make it carry.

The physiotherapy department was in the cinema. A large board in the foyer displayed the time-table for a whole week, including classes for three grades of specialised remedial exercises and treatments, as well as periods for occupational therapy, swimming and walking. The miners could use the one functioning golf course, and in the warmer weather we played bowls and took the exercise classes on the lawns.

The ballroom was equipped for badminto[n]. When the shuttle-cock flew over the woode[n] partition at one end, and we climbed over [to] retrieve it, the sight of the huge pile of store[d] carpets was impressive—and explained th[e] strong smell of moth-balls!.

We had a party in the ballroom. The miners ha[d] a preference for circle waltzes, which suited m[e] but I wasn't used to being left abruptly high an[d] dry and a little unsteady in the middle of the floo[r]. No gallantries!

More in the ceilidh tradition, the M.C. woul[d] announce that "Mr X will now entertain the com[pany]"—whereupon Mr X would stand up an[d] burst into a song or recitation where he stood. [I] found myself joining in the chorus of "The Britis[h] Working Man" under the chandeliers [of] Gleneagles Hotel!

Sleeping accommodation for the miners was o[n] the first floor, where the larger suites had bee[n] turned into dormitories. The brighter spark[s] played pranks, and apple-pie beds were a ne[w] experience for some of these middle-aged me[n]. They came from all over the Scottish coalfield[s] and were not the top earners that they are toda[y]. They were then serving the war effort in [a] reserved and dangerous occupation, which had [a] high accident and injury rate. Their ages range[d] from 17 to 70.

Our accommodation was on the third floor. W[e] had single rooms, furnished with the heavy, goo[d] quality furniture of the period, and a choice [of] bathrooms along the corridor. The old-fashione[d] plumbing meant that you could lose wash-clot[hs] and soap down the enormous plug hole if yo[u] didn't watch out.

The suites served as sitting rooms. The femal[e] paramedics shared, and my most vivid memory i[s] of hair-drying sessions in front of the electric ba[r]

Page left: 1920's trio at the hotel from left: George Alexander, head greenkeeper; Frank C. Fisher, resident manager; J.M. Barclay, secretary, Golfers are the Cowan Dobsons. Above: Neville Chamberlain. Many of the hotel guests in 1939 recall listening to the Prime Minister's speech (as did millions of others all over Britain) declaring the outbreak of war, as crowds gathered outside No. 10 Downing Street.

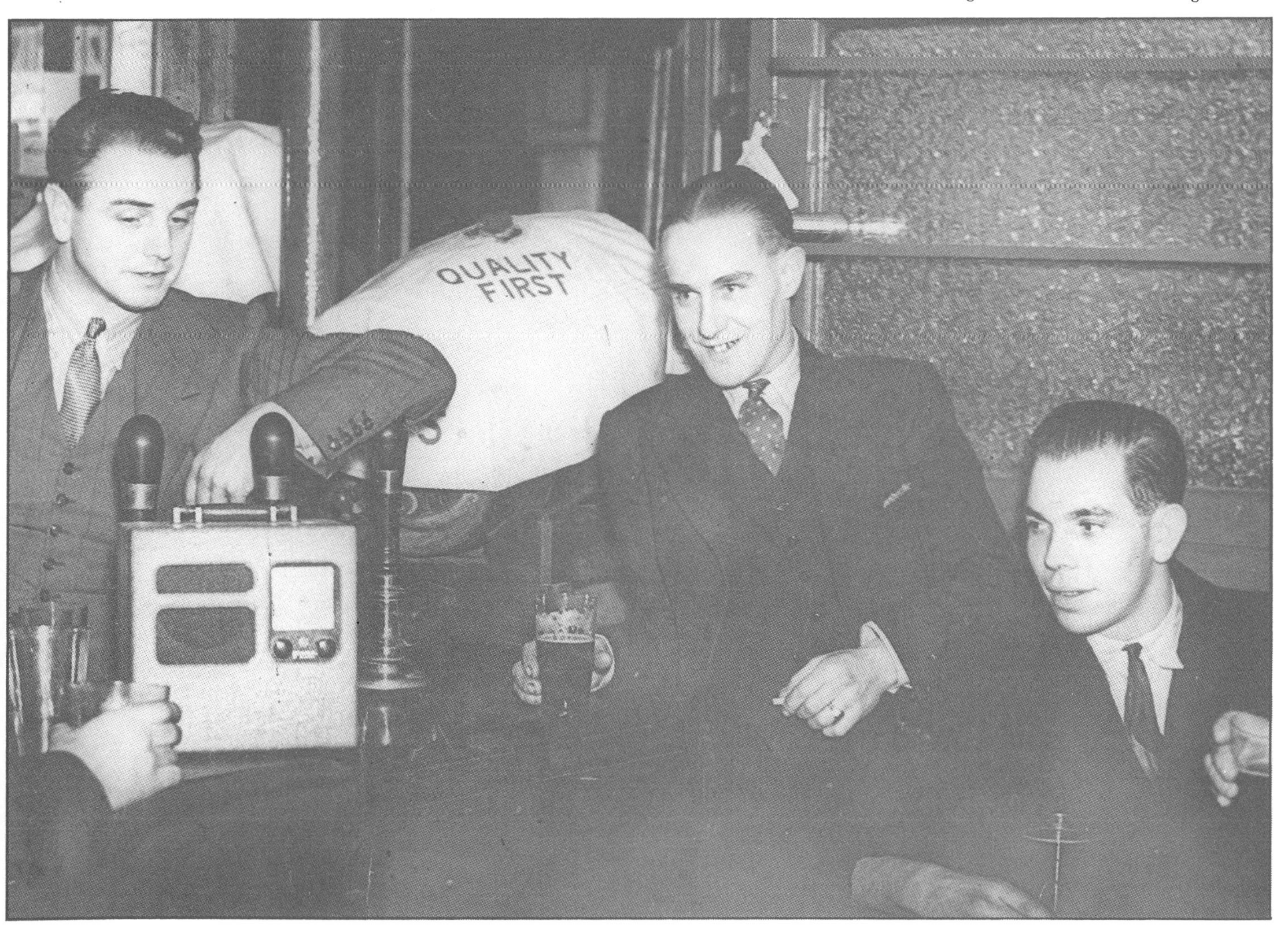

fires. My colleagues were quite a dazzling lot. One, the Canadian occupational therapist, was a handsome girl with waist-length hair. A physiotherapist had glorious red hair, and the radiographer was a striking, genuine blonde. I was the mousy one.

My bedroom was over the back door—not one of the best on offer since the railway engine bringing the coal supply on the private line moved in and out just below—but I had only to raise my head from the pillow to see the view of moor and mountain.

The Red Cross ran a library in the French restaurant, and a canteen for cocoa and Horlicks in the little service area near the foyer. We volunteered our services for that. The library was manned by a charming member of the Haldane family from Gleneagles House.

Alcohol was in short supply and the miners soon exhausted the stocks of the Dormie House. It had to be closed, and the miners then resorted to taxis to take them to Auchterarder.

We borrowed bicycles to get to the shops. In constant searches for hard-to-find cosmetics, we discovered a chemist who made up his own brand of face-cream and had occasional stocks of Innoxa and Nivea—new names to us then. (I now can never drive through Auchterarder without that particular smell coming back to me.)

Once, we had a death—one of the miners—and all the others insisted on the traditional right to a day off work and a slow parade behind the hearse to the main gates.

Why did I leave? It was a lovely experience, but I was young and wanted to volunteer for India. I could hardly save on a salary of £190 per annum!—(Mrs.) H.J.PRICE, Edinburgh.

DOROTHY CRAWFORD, now retired and living in London, spent a great deal of time at Gleneagles Hotel—first as an assistant at L.M.S. headquarters, working from St Pancras Station in London, and latterly as Decoration and Furnishing Manager for British Transport Hotels, until 1975. Still full of nostalgia for "The Glen"—as it was known to the hotel staff—she contributes this graphic account of how the hotel came to be reopened after the Second World War, and some of the memorable personalities concerned in that mammoth operation.

AFTERMATH OF WAR —THE PHOENIX RISES

I had been to Gleneagles Hotel before the 1939-45 war as a visitor, never dreaming that I would have such a long association with it in the future. My business association began in 1946 when, as assistant to the L.M.S. company's Officer for Domestic Services, I went with my colleague Min Carswell to make a preliminary inspection of the furnishings stored since the day the hotel closed in 1939 "for the duration."

On a dark December day we started unsealing stores, opening out pairs of curtains, inspecting carpets, deciding on renewals. The engineer-in-charge, James MacMillan, had guarded the place as his own and virtually no deterioration had taken place during the seven years or so between packing up and now. After this first visit, through January, February and March, the planning and organising went on. The Ministry of Health finally vacated the upper floors and the army of workmen moved in.

That winter was the worst I remember. Snow lay two feet deep in places. The frozen snow was dangerous underfoot and the walk to the club house for a meal was not pleasant. The Superintendent loaned us cars to get to and from the station a mile away. One day all the cars were stuck in the snow and I had to struggle down the hill up to my knees with every step I took.

The little engine that pulled the goods train up through the heather and right under the canopy at the hotel's back door was kept busy. Train times to Edinburgh were checked and it was found that the morning train from Perth had stopped the extra three minutes at Gleneagles Station all through the war, although no hotel laundry van was there to be attached. No alteration in timetables was needed.

The painters arrived, some of the original wallpapers from 1924 were still on the walls and acceptable till austerity was over. (Strathearn has lovely clean air). One hazard was the snow. Paint colours chosen when the ground outside is white look very different when green grass shows again. Materials were in short supply. Only the purple repp curtains from 1924 were relegated to staff. (I vowed the day would come when staff got new furnishings and not cast-offs—and they did before I retired).

Left: Playing in the haggis. The traditional ceremony took place in 1949 at a 51st Highland Division reunion dinner. Above: first dance of the new season was an occasion to bring out the clan tartans and the ball gowns. Below: the staff, traditionally part of the 'family' often took part in sports and games on special days.

I REMEMBER GLENEAGLES HOTEL...

I remember the night the first sitting room—number 222—was fit to sit in. It had a Jacobean suite with a leather studded table and a sideboard the shape of a coffin. What was meant to be a candle-lit meeting with the Superintendent and the matron somehow turned into a séance—both were of Highland origin. There were power cuts all the time, so the walk back to our bedrooms, tripping over rolls of carpet, avoiding loose floorboards and electric wires, was indeed a spooky experience.

Power cuts caused many problems. New carpet for the second floor corridor was made at a rate of twelve yards a day, using electricity when it was available. The corridor is a quarter of a mile long. We got the carpet just in time.

All during the war my chief had been contemplating the reopening and buying anything she thought worthy of Gleneagles. There was a fine Georgian chandelier bought at an auction in Belgrave Square for the smokeroom, and real French silk brocades and damasks for chair coverings. A designer called Anne Loosely printed her own designs on plain material, notably for the dining room. This took 300 yards.

The bedroom suites needed little attention, but the polishers were happy with the change from polishing coffins. The Chinese suite furniture needed repainting. One of the painters, from Glasgow, did no bad job on the little Chinese figures. With the arrival of lampshades to replace the hand-painted shades of 1924, we began to feel we were getting somewhere.

The mural artist Beatrice MacDermott was engaged to paint panels in the lounge—King Robert the Bruce and de Bohun, and Bruce and the Red Comyn—and depict folkloric legends over the fireplaces on the landings.

About the beginning of March, when the Ministry of Health departed and the snow melted, the Heads of Department began to come back from the hotels where they had spent the war. Most were extremely pleased. Gleneagles Hotel was, after all, a way of life!

Étienne Cottet, the first manager in 1947, was Swiss. He had done part of his training in the dining room before the war and knew the hotel and its clientèle well. His enthusiasm was infectious. He was approachable and full of humour. His wartime service at Euston and the Adelphi in Liverpool during the blitz and later at the Midland, Manchester, made him the senior manager.

The housekeeper, however, had never been in a seasonal hotel and was used to a settled routine. When the Head Plateman (who doubled as First Aid man) was called upon to deliver a baby girl the morning the hotel opened—the still room maid *had* seemed rather on the stout side—Miss O'Callaghan was heard to mutter as she fled the scene: "It would *never* have happened at Manchester!"

Chef Newhouse was also Swiss. He, too, had been in Liverpool. He had a dry sense of humour. He it was who gazed at Mrs MacDermott working on a mural and, when she explained that she had to paint the figure nude before putting in the draperies, gave a Gallic shrug and said': "Why bother? Plain cabbage is best!"

Monsieur Labarbe, the fish chef, was noted for his habit of taking out his glass eye and laying it down beside the fish.

Joe Bertelli was the first of a long line of Maîtres d'Hotel. His spiderlike movements were reminiscent of Max Wall, but he would work harder than any of his staff when it came to setting up a banquet or clearing it away. Harry Walton was the Head Barman when the hotel reopened. He came from Manchester, where he wintered. Later, Duncan MacMillan had one of the best jobs: six months at Gleneagles, one month's holiday and five at Charing Cross. He was very well known to the guests.

Just as waiters tended to be Italian, Head Porters started as page boys. Davy Gordon was another who spent the time when Gleneagles was closed at the Liverpool Adelphi. He was a genial man, always with a smile and a joke.

These, and many more men and women who had worked at "The Glen" before the war, came back and took up their posts as if they had never been away. Each set his own department to rights. Towards the opening date the junior staff were pressed into service to help the gang of labourers, and they were joined by German prisoners of war from the camp at Comrie. The prisoners seemed to enjoy the change of work and did a roaring trade selling slippers made of rushes collected from the district.

Once we came down to the ground floor the pressure was truly on. In the ballroom the crystal chandeliers were uncovered and found to be intact, although the room had been used as a gymnasium both by the R.A.F. and by the miners who were the last occupants. When the fittings were taken down for cleaning someone stole some of the beads, thinking they had some value. Chambermaids came back and put their rooms to rights. They knew every piece of furniture and ornament and where it had been in 1939.

There were two shops on the ground floor—Rowan's of Glasgow and Madame Galin's salon. Madame Galin, a Russian refugee in 1918, had opened a salon in Dover Street in London. Her speciality was a cashmere made for her exclusively in the Borders, and from it she made suits and coats which were timeless. For many years until at least the late sixties, Hélène Galin sold her classic outfits to wealthy women. They saw, admired, enquired for them in London, but found they could not get them anywhere else and wrote to Madame. She was one of the great characters who made Gleneagles Hotel special. Like her clothes, she seemed ·ageless and indestructible.

One of the most vital members of the staff was the hotel telephonist, Moira Cowie, who had previously worked there for the Ministry of Health.* She stayed on to become the hotel's link with the world. Her skill and charm in dealing with international calls made her popular with guests and management alike.

The only hotel post office in Scotland re-opened.

The night before the whole hotel opened the manager made his tour of inspection. Two unexpected American guests then arrived—and were admitted—they not realising we were not officially ready for business. This fact had to be hidden from one of the regular pre-war visitors, Mrs Hay, who was waiting on the doorstep to be "the first", as she and her husband had been for many years before the war. It would have been such a shame to spoil her pleasure.

At 10.30 on the opening day in April, 1947, Étienne Cottet gathered his staff (all beautifully garbed in new uniforms) in the ballroom, gave them a pep talk and declared the hotel open.

I have mentioned Mrs Hay. There were many other "regulars". Well known and well liked. Among the most memorable was undoubtedly Lady Gamage. She was an institution. With her husband, Sir Leslie, she spent the month of August at Gleneagles for many years.

As in every hotel the housekeeper had a book where guests' requirements were noted. Most were simple to arrange—an extra pillow, another lamp, more blankets, or less, and so on. Lady Gamage requested occasional tables—lots of them. Thus all the other suites were denuded when she visited the hotel. A plan was made so that each table would be in just the correct place. After a few years money for furnishing was easier to come by and extra small tables were bought specially for her.

There was a great good-humoured rivalry amongst the "regulars." If one found that another had been given new cushions or a new carpet he wanted to know why *he* had nothing new.

Jealousy reached a fine pitch when one American millionaire sent an ultimatum that if his suite was not completely refurbished when he arrived in three weeks' time, that would be the end of his patronage. A carpet was specially woven, the rooms were decorated, new curtains, lampshades, cushions—everything! He was delighted, but the management had a hard time with certain other regular guests...

Now and again, in the palmy days before the last war, the hotel found itself overbooked, and staff were astonished to find their bedrooms had been let. Once the tables were turned on the manager, Mr Pittolo, when the receptionist let *his* suite. He saw the ironic justice and laughed, but his wife did not!

This same Mr Pittolo would have done anything to please (and gently tease) the guests. On one occasion he had strawberries flown from warmer climes, tied to gooseberry bushes, to show two Spanish ladies what a wonderful climate Scotland had and that the bad weather they were experiencing was unusual for the time of year.

Last but not least of the indications of the sort of place Gleneagles Hotel was and is, there was a tradition, as in all L.M.S. hotels at that time, that the manager wore a red carnation in his buttonhole. Two were always provided by the florist in case one wilted before the end of the day.—DOROTHY CRAWFORD, Baker Street, London.

**Moira Cowie is still at Gleneagles as Head Telephonist in 1984.*

Palace on rails

A WARTIME railway car used by Mr Churchill was turned into a miniature Indian Palace last night to carry the Nawab and Begum of Bhopal to Gleneagles for six weeks' grouse shooting.

Four engraved silver spittoons, a large cloth bundle of betel nuts, a block of ice, six red-and-orange-striped cushions and bright-hued silk and brocade bedding were among the baggage taken on board.

Most of the luggage for the party of nine had been sent in advance, but they took 45 pieces of baggage with them, including the Begum's tartan shopping bag.

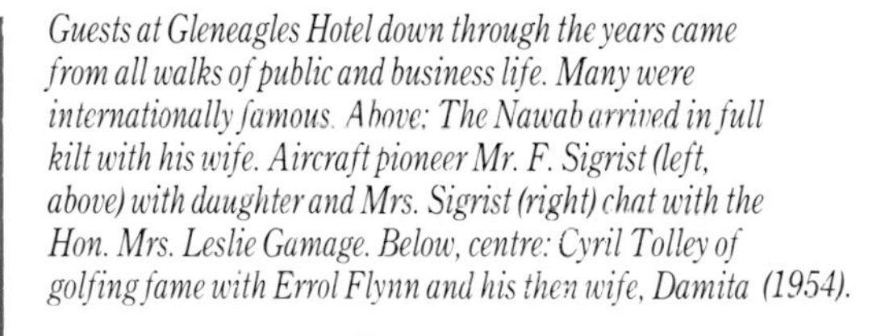

Guests at Gleneagles Hotel down through the years came from all walks of public and business life. Many were internationally famous. Above: The Nawab arrived in full kilt with his wife. Aircraft pioneer Mr. F. Sigrist (left, above) with daughter and Mrs. Sigrist (right) chat with the Hon. Mrs. Leslie Gamage. Below, centre: Cyril Tolley of golfing fame with Errol Flynn and his then wife, Damita (1954).

E P I L O G U E

Pro-celebrity golf tournaments at Gleneagles, televised on the BBC, have popularised the game for millions of non-players. Ian Wooldridge reminisces about the great names of golf and showbusiness who have helped make pro-celebrity golf a classic

In the beginning there were Tom Weiskopf and Peter Oosterhuis, who really could play golf, and a bunch of guys who thought or hoped they could. These, in that inaugural year of 1974, included Christopher Lee, fresh from his latest Ruritanian blood-lust session, Henry Cooper, of the famed left-hook, Jimmy Tarbuck, of the rapier wit, Bobby Charlton, everybody's favourite footballer, and Ronnie Corbett, of the lack of inches.

It was, of course, an outrageous idea: you teamed a famous American professional golfer with a well-known face and turned them loose on an historic Scottish golf course to play against a famous British professional golfer and another well-known face. You filmed all the matches for subsequent BBC 2 Television and called it Pro-Celebrity Golf.

The purists, make no mistake about it, were offended. You could hear them at it in the bar the following Sunday "Jesus", they'd say, "did you see Ronnie Corbett top that five-iron 20 yards? For God's sake, *I* can play better than that."

Exactly. That was precisely what was intended. When Ken Bowden first took the idea to the BBC he was lucky to run into Aubrey Singer, a man to whom golf was by no means a surrogate religion. Singer backed his own heretical judgement.

"I'm looking for a programme", he said, "which will broaden golf's appeal, something which will get the whole family involved. I don't want all that business about 'level fours'. I want a straight-forward head-to-head match where absolutely everyone can understand what the hell's going on."

At first it seemed that even the Almighty didn't agree with the concept. They meant to film ten matches at Turnberry, on the Ayrshire coast, but quit after seven. It blew a force-ten gale for most of the week and rained in stair rods. Dear Fred MacMurray, then 66, was paired with Weiskopf against Oosterhuis and Bobby Charlton and, in conditions more like the rounding of Cape Horn than a golf match in a Scottish holiday resort, there were grave doubts at one stage whether MacMurray's failing health would stand it, Characteristically he battled on.

It was five months before that match hit the screens of BBC Television. Then, a few days later, the audience viewing returns came in. *Four million,* a large figure anyway for BBC 2 but a phenomenal one for an experimental golf match, had switched over to watch. Pro-Celebrity Golf was home and dry.

The following year, in the hope of better weather inland, the circus moved to Gleneagles, with its three courses (then) set among the romantic rolling hills of Perthshire. It was the start of a stupendous relationship. That year the celebrities included Bing Crosby and Howard Keel from America with Dickie Henderson and Charlie Drake representing British wit and James Hunt, the Grand Prix racing driver, outraging everyone by turning out in his favourite sartorial condition which is roughly equivalent to that of a super-annuated scarecrow.

"Well", recalls Slim Wilkinson, the BBC's Pro-Celebrity Golf producer of those early days, "we couldn't lay down the law about dress standards. The celebrities aren't paid, of course, What the BBC could offer them was a stay in the lovely hotel and golf for a week. They loved it."

So did the BBC. Every man, as we know, has his price. There are some things that money cannot buy. It can certainly buy a week's golf at Gleneagles, but it cannot buy a week's golf at Gleneagles televised not only for British viewing but for distribution around the world. If you have any brains at all you do not knock back an invitation to play in Pro-Celebrity Golf. Crying 'I love ya baby' at every opportunity, Telly Savalas was the first to realise that.

Within three years it had settled down as one of the most sophisticated sports TV programmes in the world. It could beckon, on the celebrity side, damn nearly anyone. In 1976 professionals Johnny Miller and Tony Jacklin were joined by, among others, Sean 'James Bond' Connery, Val Doonican and beautifully dressed as always, another Grand Prix driver named Jackie Stewart. Burt Lancaster, actor emeritus, turned up, as did Alan Shepard, astronaut and moon-walker.

"The amazing thing", recalls Slim Wilkinson, "is that the stars of screen and stage and football pitch, men who had flown to the moon and back, people who had faced millions, even billions, on television, became completely different people in Pro-Celebrity golf. You could wander out there when they were practising and see them whack booming 250-yard drives straight down the middle. And yet the moment you put a television camera on them for their big match of the week, they were quite capable of cracking up. It was a terrific insight into some of them."

For one or two it was to be an insight that has never been explained. George C. Scott, incandescent actor of Patton fame, booked into the Gleneagles Hotel in 1976 and booked out again the following morning without a word of explanation.

Did he get cold feet? Someone must know the answer but none of the dozen people I asked about that extraordinary defection would even hint at the reason. Golfers, and I like them for it, are very loyal to one another.

Wilkinson got to know the celebrities as well as anyone. He is himself a fanatically keen golfer off a high handicap and so he understood, better than most, their nerves when confronted by professionals.

"Suddenly", he recalls, "you saw them stripped. Johnny Mathis on the concert platform was most certainly not Johnny Mathis on the first tee. Johnny Mathis on the first tee was you or me, in awe of the great players alongside him.

"The levelling-out process, of course, came at the end of the day. We all went back to Gleneagles Hotel and, for want of a better word, relaxed. It was an amazing atmosphere. In that company some of the biggest stars in the world of showbusiness became quite ordinary people. They didn't go around trying to impress people. It was as though golf was bigger than all of them. I guess it is."

Wilkinson recalled the very first Pro-Celebrity tournament with Fred MacMurray, who was shortly to return to America and be declared desperately ill with cancer.

"By God what guts that man had", he said. "After that terrible round in the driving rain he came into the billiard room after dinner and joined in the fun. His second wife, the actress June Haver, might have been on some club outing. Suddenly she jumped on to the piano and started singing one of the famous songs from her films. Everyone joined in. It was one of the great nights of the competition.

"As a matter of fact, that was rather an exception. It might seem hard to believe but the American celebrities were far more introverted than the British. I think they came over expecting to find Gleneagles as simple as some manicured inland American course. They had to learn the hard way. Quite a few of them were very subdued in the evenings.

"The Brits were much more relaxed. When Jimmy Tarbuck and Bruce Forsyth got together the jokes crackled around like machinegun fire. Sean Connery could be terrific, too—unless he'd lost.

"Sean's a terrific golfer, but the simple truth is that he can't stand losing. When he's won a match he's the ultimate charmer. When he loses he's a bear with worse than a sore head. He takes the whole thing very seriously indeed."

Down the years the celebrity field broadened: Test cricketer Colin Cowdrey, jockey Geoff Lewis, snooker maestro Ray Reardon, tennis star Lew Hoad, Prime Minister's offspring Mark Thatcher, actor Jack

The Red Carpet Treatment

Whether it is the latest Bentley Mulsanne Turbo, a Rolls Royce Silver Spirit or indeed any one of the range of 40 different models from which you can make your choice, you may be sure that your car will be presented to you in immaculate condition in every respect and that you will receive the personal attention and service for which we have always been renowned, in fact the Guy Salmon Red Carpet Treatment.

Our extensive self-drive fleet contains four and five seater saloons, family estates and hatchbacks, convertibles, sports cars and city runabouts, all of which have been carefully selected to give you the ultimate in choice.

With free delivery and collection within 20 miles of any branch and unlimited mileage*, our tariff is always competitive but never at the expense of the standards of service which our customers have come to expect.

At any of our nationwide network of branches you will always receive a smiling and courteous reception. You have only to call UK Central Reservations on

01-408 1255

to have at your immediate disposal . . .

Guy Salmon – The finest service in car rental

Regional reservation offices: Birmingham 021-643 4052 · Manchester 061-236 0242 · Glasgow 041-332 7979
and at Gleneagles and Caledonian Hotels

*1-2 days, 100 miles free per day.

Lemmon and a great World War Two air ace, the legless and now dead Sir Douglas Bader, joined in.

The professional field broadened, too, until by wonderful luck they found Lee Trevino. Chunky, democratic, wise-cracking, unorthodox, live-for-today Trevino stepped into Pro-Celebrity golf as little less than its resident comedian.

He is one of the reasons why such an esoteric sports programme has sustained enormously high ratings among television audiences in Britain. "What a card", say the housewives who would be hard-pressed to explain the difference between a three-iron and a garden hoe.

No-one questions Trevino's impact on his public. Few would believe his actual life-style.

He arrives at Gleneagles, unpacks his bags, is scrupulously polite to all his fans and wildly generous by way of tips and Christian-name recognition to all the staff. On course he is as spontaneously witty as Tarbuck or Ronnie Corbett. But as soon as the cameras are switched off he becomes his own man again.

"If you had to pick out one man who'd be the life and soul of the party that evening", said a witness who is going to remain absolutely anonymous, "I guess you'd pick out Lee. Not a bit of it. When his game is over he comes back to the hotel, has one beer with his friends to be sociable and then just disappears to his room. He has dinner up there and watches television all on his own. That, I guess, is why he's the ultimate professional."

That, in fact, is not wholly true.

Trevino is an ice-cream freak. Throughout the week of the Pro-Celebrity tournament he receives a daily supply of ice-cream from a friend in Glasgow and once, during the week, he gets his mate over to Gleneagles and entertains him to dinner. "That", says the observer, "is about the only time we see him except on the final night. Some man, that Trevino. We all respect him enormously."

The voice of the Pro-Celebrity event on the box, of course, is that of Peter Alliss, a superbly gifted but largely unfulfilled professional golfe whose easy manner and command of the swiftly spoken word have, within five years, made him one of the most impressive sports commentators in the English Language.

What is so admirable about Alliss is that he has not fallen for the amateur journalist's dreadful habit of praising everything that his eye encompasses.

For example he doesn't give us any showbusiness rubbish at all abou the time he set out to interview Burt Lancaster at Gleneagles. "He was very courteous," says Peter, "but difficult." What Alliss was trying to get Lancaster to confirm was a very well known story: that the famous actor had become so besotted by golf at one stage that he had let his career slip and run into financial trouble.

Alliss put the proposition to Lancaster in many different ways. "No" said Lancaster every time. "In the end", recalls Alliss, "I gave up on him."

I admire Alliss, also, for refusing to go along with all the gloss. "Som of the celebrities, I'm afraid", reveals the commentator in his autobiography, "took liberties with the hospitality."

He cites, without naming names, some who were so mean that they stuck on their hotel bill Mars bars and packets of tee-pegs from the professional's shop, not to mention a la carte meals and bottles of Dom Perignon. Perhaps it would have been better if he *had* named names since the reader would not be wondering now which of his or her heroe could be so tight-fisted.

But against the whole panorama of Pro-Celebrity Golf that is but a small abberration. The game is here to stay. The nation indeed much c the world, is tuning in. A Tarbuck wisecrack superimposed on a Trevi one-iron off the fairway is, after all, a bonus not to be ignored.

Val Doonican, Bing Crosby and Tom Weiskopf, at a pro-celeb tournament.

GENERAL MANAGERS AT GLENEAGLES HOTEL

1924	F.C. Fisher
1932 – 1934	C. Pittolo
1935 – 1937	R. Nichols
1938 – 1939	C. Pittolo
1947 – 1948	E.R. Cottet
1949 – 1951	F.R. Collins
1952 – 1954	H.A. Berry
1955	D.A.V. Aldridge
1956	H.A. Berry
1957 – 1963	D.A.V. Aldridge
1964	I.M. Jack
1965	I.M. Jack
	V.P.R. Woodcock
1966	V.P.R. Woodcock
1967 – 1969	D.A.V. Aldridge
1970 – 1982	J.K.S. Bannatyne MBE
1982 – 1984	G.G. Macpherson
1984	P.J. Lederer